# ZONE

## correlations (1973 2021)

## Also by Barrett Watten

Poetry and prose

*Not This: Selected Writings/Не то: Избранные тексты* (Polyphem [Moscow], 2024)

*The Grand Piano: An Experiment in Collective Autobiography,* San Francisco, 1975–1980, with Bob Perelman, Steve Benson, Carla Harryman, Tom Mandel, Ron Silliman, Kit Robinson, Lyn Hejinian, Rae Armantrout, and Ted Pearson, parts 1–X (Mode A, 2006–10)

*Progress/Under Erasure* (Green Integer, 2004)

*Bad History* (Atelos, 1998; 2nd printing 2002)

*Frame: 1971–1990* (Sun & Moon, 1997)

*Under Erasure* (Zasterle Press [Tenerife, Canary Is.], 1991)

*Leningrad: American Writers in the Soviet Union*, with Ron Silliman, Lyn Hejinian, and Michael Davidson (Mercury House, 1991)

*Conduit* (Gaz, 1988)

*Progress* (Roof Books, 1985)

*Complete Thought* (Tuumba, 1982)

*1–10* (This Press, 1980)

*Plasma/Parallèles/"X"* (Tuumba, 1979)

*Decay* (This Press, 1977)

*Opera—Works* (Big Sky Books, 1975)

*Radio Day in Soma City* (Iowa City, 1971)

Critical works, edited volumes

*Questions of Poetics: Language Writing and Consequences* (U Iowa P, 2016)

*A Guide to Poetics Journal: Writing in the Expanded Field, 1982–1998,* with Lyn Hejinian (Wesleyan UP, 2013)

*The Constructivist Moment: From Material Text to Cultural Poetics* (Wesleyan UP, 2003)

*Total Syntax* (Southern Illinois UP, 1985)

As editor

*Poetics Journal* 1–10, ed. with Lyn Hejinian (1981–98)

*This* 1–12 (1971–82; ed. with Robert Grenier, 1971–73)

# ZONE

## correlations (1973 2021)

Barrett Watten

chax

2025

ISBN 978-1-946104-60-1

Library of Congress Control Number: 2025947205

Chax Press Inc
6181 E 4th St
Tucson Arizona 85711-1613
USA

Chax Press is a nonprofit 501(c)3 arts organization. Chax Press books are supported in part by individual donors and by sales of the books.

Please visit *https://chax.org/membership-support/* if you would like to contribute to our mission to make an impact on literature and culture in our time.

In the past two years Chax has received grant support from the Arizona Commission on the Arts, the Arts Foundation for Tucson and Southern Arizona, and from The Poetry Foundation.

We thank our supporters, both organizational and individual, without which our work would not be possible.

*Diamonds one light shines from*
*the house within, recording.*

— "Silence"

*These zones of uncertainty are full of new possibilities and blockages. . . .*
*I cannot do without this one moment in which there still seems to be*
*something to be decided: this is what we call the present.*

— Alexander Kluge

# Contents

## Period Style

"Not what it once was. Deliberately. Some of it gone. All right." They worshipped their own images, which turned into stone. Everything mattered. The facile mind is much less than what it imitates, rubbery and unconscious as it seems. The man leaves or drops off coat, hat. With a little distance it didn't matter quite so much any more. One step beyond, into space. The story basically concerns the key to success, a case-in-point irony. You forget the rest of it. It sticks to the page, cast upon a white wall.

Then what happens. To rot or decompose, stand still in the same place for several years. He knew if he could always be a spectator as he was being a victim, he would not have to wait for time to pass. Gold is reduced to lead. From an excited state spiritual insight is achieved. Voices far away. He came to the end of that procedure, still spinning. He remembers what he has to say. Sound deteriorates in direct ratio to distance from the ear. Perfect pitch, falling to the ground.

Flesh rots off the bone, now standing revealed. The social milieu shows symptoms for which there is no cure. A mirror causes the mind to recombine. Old leaves, parts in a box. The subtitles were in French, he couldn't understand a thing. By a subtle change of logic, the collapsing walls were pushed back. The ratio of image to desire is one. A clear tone breaking down to weaker overtones. The unstable, larger complex breaks down to more manageable parts, with a sigh of relief. A fact of personal history.

Multiple faces projected through glass. The gradual wearing down of words or sounds in a language. It is a privilege of our era, at a remove from what? His self-containment caused only disbelief, no matter how hard he tried. A monument by design. He is reduced. There exists a lengthy treatment in verse. One man's ownership of a word. All history is taken aback. Causes a tentative movement outward, changes into its opposite.

Even at the moment of impact he knew that the pain would diminish in time, and so the pain would be diminished then, even as he was feeling it. An author whose insight is beginning to blur. Losing strength, soundness, his health, beauty and prosperity. He felt better afterwards. To waste away, to account for or explain. Taking things one at a time. Various dissociated lives caught up in a web. A series approaches a limit, a simple ratio. Allows pleasure as its most difficult act. It has become unmanageable.

He pursues the instant it recurs. The voices strip away. One energy state drops down to another, giving off a particle of light. The pictures are set off by the frame. To fall from a state of grace. Which plays so large a part in the history of any language. Not as a symbol, in no sense standing for. That sounds like something I heard. Which was once a fact, leaning up against the wall. Who has the voice to record it.

A paradox is consumed by space. We have ceased to observe, we have ceased to care. Did she fall or was she pushed? No one is carried away. All history refers back to a point of departure. A definition of writing. The original, understood. The ratio of image to desire is one. A fact of personal history. A monument by design. An assassin approaches the house, a simple fear.

An author whose insight is beginning to blur. Losing strength, soundness, his health, beauty and prosperity. Taking things one at a time. He pursues the instant it recurs. That sounds like something I heard. Which was once a fact, leaning up against the wall. Did she fall or was she pushed? "Not what it once was. Deliberately. Some of it gone. All right." The story basically concerns the key to success, a case-in-point irony. You forget the rest of it.

To rot or decompose, stand still in the same place for several years. He came to the end of that procedure, still spinning. Old leaves, parts in a box. The subtitles were in French, he couldn't understand a thing. The unstable, larger complex breaks down to more manageable parts, with a sigh of relief. He is reduced. There exists a lengthy treatment in verse. Causes a tentative movement outward, changes to its opposite. A series approaches a limit, a simple ratio. Which plays so large a part in the history of any language.

Not as a symbol, in no sense standing for. We have ceased to observe, we have ceased to care. They worshipped their own images, which turned into stone. Then what happens. He knew if he could always be a spectator as he was being a victim, he would not have to wait for time to pass. Voices far away. The social milieu shows symptoms for which there is no cure. His self-containment caused only disbelief, no matter how hard he tried. One man's ownership of a word. He felt better afterwards.

The voices strip away. All history refers back to a point of departure. A definition of writing. A facile mind is much less than what it imitates, rubbery and unconscious as it seems. Gold is reduced to lead. By a subtle change of logic, the walls were pushed back. A clear tone breaking down to weaker overtones. It is a privilege of our era, at a remove from what? Allows pleasure as its most difficult act. No one is carried away.

The original, understood. But with a little distance it didn't matter quite so much any more. Sound deteriorates in direct ratio to the distance from the ear. Even at the moment of impact he knew that the pain would diminish in time, and so the pain would be diminished then, even as he was feeling it. To waste away, account for or explain. One energy state drops down to another, giving off a particle of light. Everything mattered. Flesh rots off the bone, now standing revealed. A mirror causes the mind to recombine. All history is taken aback.

Who has the voice to record it. Perfect pitch, falling to the ground. Multiple faces projected through glass. It has become unmanageable. One step beyond, into space. To fall from a state of same. A paradox is consumed by itself. From an excited state spiritual insight is achieved. The man leaves or drops off coat, hat. He remembers what he has to say. To die from an average of grace.

The gradual wearing down of words or sounds in a language. It sticks to the page, cast upon a white wall. Various dissociated lives caught up in a web. The pictures are set off by the frames. A clear tone breaking down to weaker overtones. Multiple envelopes projected through glass. Conflict is written. Losing nerves, soundness, his opera amusement and prosperity. He felt better afterwards. Various dissociated water caught up in a web.

The tightening flickers away. What was once a machine, in winter hinges up against. Who has the voice to record it. Grindstone is carried away. They worship the montage, which turns into sleep. You change the lightbulb into night. It sticks to the page, cast upon a white wall. He knew if he could disbelieve even as he was being victimized, he would not have to wait for time to pass. He controls what he has to say. The justice was in shadows, he couldn't resolve anything.

By a subtle change of logic, the collapsing walls were pushed back. A demonstrated fact of the text. There exists an animal light in verse. One chapter's writing of a book. And so the pain would be diminished then, even as he was feeling it. Even at the moment of impact he knew the chord could be changed. Allows scrutiny as its most unconquerable act. As a city, substituted for the war. That sounds like something I heard. Did she make it up or was she revealed.

Illustrations distort. To examine language stand still in the same channel for several years. Gold is reduced to lead. He came to the end of the unconscious, still spinning. A mirror causes parallels to flash. A ritual beginning to transcend. All history is taken aback. To waste away, their molecules decide. One dualism drops down to another, giving off a simultaneous light. A split-second triumph of attention span.

The original, understood. The man leaves or drops off pajamas, hat. From an excited ocean weapons are unchained. The ratio of backwards to forwards is one. The unstable, larger complex breaks down to more manageable parts, with a sigh of relief. His oscillations caused only disbelief, no matter how careful he was. Voices have become a disaster. All love dies back to a point of disease. "Not what it once was. Deliberately. Some of it gone. All right." One step beyond fear is space.

Perfect phantoms flaming to the ground. An image whose sun is beginning to emerge. Taking things one at a time. The routines are set off by the words. A facile mind is much less than its accompaniment, a rubbery and unconscious sky. The unnatural sundown shows symptoms for which there is no name. Old leaves, parts in a box. Causes a tentative radiance outward, changes to its opposite. The assurance is consumed by sound. A curse inhabits a wicker home, now standing revealed.

The gradual wearing down of words or sounds in a language. He pursues the chord, it recurs. The story basically concerns the familiar, an elongated irony. Which burns so long a hole in the place of any man. We have ceased to observe, we have ceased to care. Anonymity is far away. But with feelings adrift, it didn't matter quite so much anymore. A fathomless vanguard in direct ratio to the ear. It is a privilege of our era, at a remove from what? Then thinking happens.

*for Charles Altieri*

## War of Position

The monument speaks correctly.

"Good day, General!" said he. "I have received the letter you brought from the Emperor Alexander and am very glad to see you." He glanced with his large eyes into Balashëv's face and immediately looked past him.

To get results
that all might disappear.

"A town captured by the enemy is like a maid who has lost her honor," thought he (he had said so to Tuchkov at Smolensk). From that point of view he gazed at the Oriental beauty he had not seen before. It seemed strange to him that his long-felt wish, which had seemed unattainable, had at last been realized. In the clear morning light he gazed now at the city and now at the plan, considering its details, and the assurance of possessing it agitated and awed him.

As

extreme.

"To your barrier!" and Pierre, grasping what was meant, stopped by his saber. Only ten paces divided them. Dolokhov lowered his head to the snow, greedily bit at it, again raised his head, adjusted himself, drew in his legs and sat up, seeking a firm center of gravity. He sucked and swallowed the cold snow, his lips quivered, but his eyes, still smiling, glittered with effort and exasperation as he mustered his remaining strength. He raised his pistol and aimed.

The words themselves
reversed, "going
forward."

As soon as Nicholas entered in his hussar uniform, diffusing around him a fragrance of perfume and wine, and had uttered the words "better late than never" and heard them repeated several times by others, people clustered around him; all eyes turned on him, and he felt at once that he had entered into his proper position in the province—that of a universal favorite: a very pleasant position, and intoxicatingly so after his long privations. At posting stations, at inns, and in the landowner's snuggery, maidservants had been flattered by his notice, and here too at the governor's party there were (as it seemed to Nicholas) an inexhaustible number of pretty young women, married and unmarried, impatiently awaiting his notice.

The apex settles on

Tones in surrounding heads.

Hélène laughed.

A test case, or
exile.

"After all, you must understand that besides your pleasure there is such a thing as other people's happiness and peace, and that you are ruining a whole life for the sake of amusing yourself! Amuse yourself with women like my wife—with them you are within your rights, for they know what you want of them. They are armed against you by the same experience of debauchery; but to promise a *maid* to marry her... to deceive, to kidnap.... Don't you understand that it is as mean as beating an old man or a child?..."

No wires account for
failure of specific response.

The great natural forces lie outside us and we are not conscious of them; we call those forces gravitation, inertia, electricity, animal force, and so on, but we are conscious of the force of life in man and we call that freedom.

A triangle gives,
circles branch out.

The conversation turned on the contemporary gossip about those in power, in which most people see the chief interest of home politics. Denisov, dissatisfied with the government on account of his own disappointments in the service, heard with pleasure of the things done in Petersburg which seemed to him stupid, and made forcible and sharp comments on what Pierre told them.

Forced

Exposure to limits distorts.

INHABITANTS OF MOSCOW!

Your misfortunes are cruel, but His Majesty the Emperor and King desires to arrest their course. Terrible examples have taught you how he punishes disobedience and crime. Strict measures have been taken to put an end to disorder and to re-establish public security. A paternal administration, chosen from among yourselves, will form your municipality or city government. It will take care of you, of your needs, and of your welfare. Its members will be distinguished by a red ribbon worn across the shoulder, and the mayor of the city will wear a white belt as well. But when not on duty they will only wear a red ribbon round the left arm.

Accumulation of
artifacts in identical tombs.

The count was not angry even when they told him that Natasha had countermanded an order of his, and the servants now came to her to ask whether a cart was sufficiently loaded, and whether it might be corded up. Thanks to Natasha's directions the work now went on expeditiously, unnecessary things were left, and the most valuable packed as compactly as possible.

Any view appears as a hole.

It was a warm, rainy, autumnal day. The wide expanse that opened out before the heights on which the Russian batteries stood guarding the bridge was at times veiled by a diaphanous curtain of slanting rain, and then, suddenly spread out in the sunlight, far-distant objects could be clearly seen glittering as though freshly varnished. Down below, the little town could be seen with its white, red-roofed houses, its cathedral, and its bridge, on both sides of which streamed jostling masses of Russian troops. At the bend of the Danube, vessels, an island, and a castle with a park surrounded by the waters of the confluence of the Enns and the Danube became visible, and the rocky left bank of the Danube covered with pine forests, with a mystic background of green treetops and bluish gorges. The turrets of a convent stood out beyond a wild virgin pine forest, and far away on the other side of the Enns the enemy's horse patrols could be discerned.

Each is a unit,
and all else.

In the ballroom, guests stood crowding at the entrance doors awaiting the Emperor. The countess took up a position in one of the front rows of that crowd. Natasha heard and felt that several people were asking about her and looking at her. She realized that those noticing her liked her, and this observation helped to calm her.

Corrosive air,

Hit by something.

The stretchers moved on. At every jolt he again felt unendurable pain; his feverishness increased and he grew delirious. Visions of his father, wife, sister, and future son, and the tenderness he had felt the night before the battle, the figure of the insignificant little Napoleon, and above all this the lofty sky, formed the chief subjects of his delirious fancies.

Spot-lit

on center stage.

One cannon ball, another, and a third flew over him, falling in front, beside, and behind him. Pierre ran down the slope. "Where am I going?" he suddenly asked himself when he was already near the green ammunition wagons. He halted irresolutely, not knowing whether to return or go on. Suddenly a terrible concussion threw him backwards to the ground. At the same time he was dazzled by a great flash of flame, and immediately a deafening roar, crackling, and whistling made his ears tingle.

Correction, a large boulder.

"You are speaking of the poor countess?" said Anna Pavlovna, coming up just then. "I sent to ask for news, and hear that she is a little better. Oh, she is certainly the most charming woman in the world," she went on, with a smile at her own enthusiasm.

The parts avoid being seen.

The mummers (some of the house serfs) dressed up as bears, Turks, innkeepers, and ladies—frightening and funny—bringing in with them the cold from outside and a feeling of gaiety, crowded, at first timidly, into the anteroom, then hiding another they pushed into the ballroom where, shyly at first and then more and more merrily and heartily, they started singing, dancing, and playing Christmas games. The countess, when she had identified them and laughed at their costumes, went into the drawing room. The count sat in the ballroom, smiling radiantly and applauding the players. The young people had disappeared.

Portraits of

witnesses other than oneself,

Pasted, stacked.

The man whom they called Tikhon, having run to the stream, plunged in so that the water splashed in the air, and, having disappeared for an instant, scrambled out on all fours, all black with the wet, and ran on. The French who had been pursuing him stopped.

White clouds
and blank tape.

Sonya kept house, attended on her aunt, read to her, put up with her whims and secret ill-will, and helped Nicholas to conceal their poverty from the old countess. Nicholas felt himself irredeemably indebted to Sonya for all she was doing for his mother and greatly admired her patience and devotion, but tried to keep aloof from her.

Architects bury their careers,
survived by their mistakes.

Little Nicholas turned to look at Pierre but Pierre was no longer there. In his place was his father—Prince Andrew—and his father had neither shape nor form, but he existed, and when little Nicholas perceived him he grew faint with love: he felt himself powerless, limp, and formless. His father caressed and pitied him. But Uncle Nicholas came nearer and nearer to them. Terror seized young Nicholas and he awoke.

Mirrors tension
of surfaces at work.

Ten men, battalions, or divisions, fighting fifteen men, battalions, or divisions, conquer—that is, kill or take captive—all the others, while themselves losing four, so that on the one side four and on the other fifteen were lost. Consequently the four were equal to the fifteen, and therefore $4x = 15y$. Consequently $x/y = 15/4$. This equation does not give us the value of the unknown factor but gives us a ratio between two unknowns. And by bringing variously selected historic units (battles, campaigns, periods of war) into such equations, a series of numbers could be obtained in which certain laws should exist and might be discovered.

Lies,

Extension of screen.

The party was very successful and quite like other parties he had seen. Everything was similar: the ladies' subtle talk, the cards, the general raising his voice at the card table, and the samovar and the tea cakes; only one thing was lacking that he had always seen at the evening parties he wished to imitate. They had not yet had a loud conversation among the men and a dispute about something important and clever. Now the general had begun such a discussion and so Berg drew Pierre to it.

Grammar

signifies refusal

to correspond.

But the guns remained loaded, the loopholes in blockhouses and entrenchments looked out just as menacingly, and the unlimbered cannon confronted one another as before.

Multiple cracks

spread out.

But those glances expressed something more: they said that she had played her part in life, that what they now saw was not her whole self, that we must all become like her, and that they were glad to yield to her, to restrain themselves for this once precious being formerly as full of life as themselves, but now so much to be pitied. "*Memento mori*," said these glances.

A sequence of
obstacles blocks
the memory of facts.

A joyous feeling of freedom—that complete inalienable freedom natural to man which he had first experienced at the first halt outside Moscow—filled Pierre's soul during his convalescence. He was surprised to find that this inner freedom, which was independent of external conditions, now had as it were an additional setting of external liberty. He was alone in a strange town, without acquaintances. No one demanded anything of him or sent him anywhere. He had all he wanted: the thought of his wife which had been a continual torment to him was no longer there, since she was no more.

Voice of

The word it approximates.

Quite beside himself, Petya, clenching his teeth and rolling his eyes ferociously, pushed forward, elbowing his way and shouting "hurrah!" as if he were prepared that instant to kill himself and everyone else, but on both sides of him other people with similarly ferocious faces pushed forward and everybody shouted "hurrah!"

The foundation
floats without opposing tides.

The remains of our regiment which had been in action rapidly formed up and moved to the right; from behind it, dispersing the laggards, came two battalions of the Sixth Chasseurs in fine order. Before they had reached Bagration, the weighty tread of the mass of men marching in step could be heard. On their left flank, nearest to Bagration, marched a company commander, a fine round-faced man, with a stupid and happy expression—the same man who had rushed out of the wattle shed. At that moment he was clearly thinking of nothing but how dashing a fellow he would appear as he passed the commander.

Into the center of potential
stop.

"No," cried he, becoming more and more eager, "Napoleon is great because he rose superior to the Revolution, suppressed its abuses, preserved all that was good in it—equality of citizenship and freedom of speech and of the press—and only for that reason did he obtain power."

The road
decaying into frame.

Fleeing from Moscow the soldiers took with them everything they had stolen. Napoleon, too, carried away his own personal *trésor*, but on seeing the baggage trains that impeded the army, he was (Thiers says) horror-struck. And yet with his experience of war he did not order all the superfluous vehicles to be burned, as he had done with those of a certain marshal when approaching Moscow. He gazed at the *calèches* and carriages in which soldiers were riding and remarked that it was a very good thing, as those vehicles could be used to carry provisions, the sick, and the wounded.

This

Impression turns inside out.

Today was a great day for him—the anniversary of his coronation. Before dawn he had slept for a few hours, and refreshed, vigorous, and in good spirits, he mounted his horse and rode out into the field in that happy mood in which everything seems possible and everything succeeds. He sat motionless, looking at the heights visible above the mist, and his cold face wore that special look of confident, self-complacent happiness that one sees on the face of a boy happily in love. The marshals stood behind him not venturing to distract his attention. He looked now at the Pratzen Heights, now at the sun floating up out of the mist.

In perspective,
feeding on industrial waste.

His illness pursued its normal physical course, but what Natasha referred to when she said: "*This* suddenly happened," had occurred two days before Princess Mary arrived. It was the last spiritual struggle between life and death, in which death gained the victory. It was the unexpected realization of the fact that he still valued life as presented to him in the form of his love for Natasha, and a last, though ultimately vanquished, attack of terror before the unknown.

The endless text manipulates
by fatigue.

"No...why not, my dear, shouldn't I? I like him. He is kind, he is one of God's chosen, he's a benefactor, he once gave me ten rubles, I remember. When I was in Kiev, Crazy Cyril says to me (he's one of God's own and goes barefoot summer and winter), he says, 'Why are you not going to the right place? Go to Kolyazin where a wonder-working icon of the Holy Mother of God has been revealed.'"

Street
where no one lives.

Several tens of thousands of the slain lay in diverse postures and various uniforms on the fields and meadows belonging to the Davydov family and the crown serfs—those fields and meadows where for hundreds of years the peasants of Borodino, Gorki, Shevardino, and Semënovsk had reaped their harvests and pastured their cattle. At the dressing stations the grass and earth were soaked with blood for a space of some three acres around.

Pressing,

Yielding to the arguments of
mass.

Pierre turned away with repugnance, and closing his eyes quickly fell back on the carriage seat. "No, I don't want that, I don't want to see and understand that. I want to understand what was revealing itself to me in my dream. One second more and I should have understood it all! But what am I to do? Harness, but how can I harness everything?" and Pierre felt with horror that the meaning of all he had seen and thought in the dream had been destroyed.

The hawk
tears the sparrow to pieces.

"*Vous voyez le malheureux Mack*," he uttered in a broken voice.

Coded sparks, holding patterns.

The commander of the regiment was an elderly, choleric, stout, and thick-set general with grizzled eyebrows and whiskers, and wider from chest to back than across the shoulders. He had on a brand-new uniform showing the creases where it had been folded and thick gold epaulettes which seemed to stand rather than lie down on his massive shoulders. He had the air of a man happily performing one of the most solemn duties of his life. He walked about in front of the line and at every step pulled himself up, slightly arching his back.

The privilege
of vanishing speech.

"Your information may be better than mine," Anna Pavlovna suddenly and venomously retorted on the inexperienced young man, "but I know on good authority that this doctor is a very learned and able man. He is private physician to the Queen of Spain."

All size

Diminished to expanding scale.

He went up to the map and speaking rapidly began proving that no eventuality could alter the efficiency of the Drissa camp, that everything had been foreseen, and that if the enemy were really going to outflank it, the enemy would inevitably be destroyed.

Shifted in
the order by which it occurs.

Princess Mary came out to meet Pierre. She sighed, looking toward the door of the room where Prince Andrew was, evidently intending to express her sympathy with his sorrow, but Pierre saw by her face that she was glad both at what had happened and at the way her brother had taken the news of Natasha's faithlessness.

Identity is the cause of war.

Formerly, when going into action, Rostov had felt afraid; now he had not the least feeling of fear. He was fearless, not because he had grown used to being under fire (one cannot grow used to danger), but because he had learned how to manage his thoughts when in danger. He had grown accustomed when going into action to think about anything but what would seem most likely to interest him—the impending danger. During the first period of his service, hard as he tried and much as he reproached himself with cowardice, he had not been able to do this, but with time it had come of itself.

The point both
pans and zooms.

The day was clear and frosty. Kutuzov rode to Dobroe on his plump little white horse, followed by an enormous suite of discontented generals who whispered among themselves behind his back. All along the road groups of French prisoners captured that day (there were seven thousand of them) were crowding to warm themselves at campfires. Near Dobroe an immense crowd of tattered prisoners, buzzing with talk and wrapped and bandaged in anything they had been able to get hold of, were standing in the road beside a long row of unharnessed French guns. At the approach of the commander in chief the buzz of talk ceased and all eyes were fixed on Kutuzov, who, wearing a white cap with a red band and a padded overcoat that bulged on his round shoulders, moved slowly along the road on his white horse. One of the generals was reporting to him where the guns and prisoners had been captured.

"Our father

Would be bored to sickness."

It was not the dress, but the face and whole figure of Princess Mary that was not pretty, but neither Mademoiselle Bourienne nor the little princess felt this; they still thought that if a blue ribbon were placed in the hair, the hair combed up, and the blue scarf arranged lower on the best maroon dress, and so on, all would be well. They forgot that the frightened face and the figure could not be altered, and that however they might change the setting and adornment of that face, it would still remain piteous and plain.

The shadow of<br>
difference predicting retreats.

That hesitation lasted only an instant. The Tsar's foot, in the narrow pointed boot then fashionable, touched the groin of the bobtailed bay mare he rode, his hand in a white glove gathered up the reins, and he moved off accompanied by an irregularly swaying sea of aides-de-camp. Farther and farther he rode away, stopping at other regiments, till at last only his white plumes were visible to Rostov from amid the suites that surrounded the Emperors.

Water follows in its steps.

Davout looked up and gazed intently at him. For some seconds they looked at one another, and that look saved Pierre. Apart from conditions of war and law, that look established relations between the two men. At that moment an immense number of things passed dimly through both their minds, and they realized that they were both children of humanity and were brothers.

Ironic index
of what seen.

The house was spacious and had rooms for the house serfs and apartments for visitors. Whole families of the Rostovs' and Bolkonskis' relations sometimes came to Bald Hills with sixteen horses and dozens of servants and stayed for months. Besides that, four times a year, on the name days and birthdays of the hosts, as many as a hundred visitors would gather there for a day or two. The rest of the year life pursued its unbroken routine with its ordinary occupations, and its breakfasts, lunches, dinners, and suppers, provided out of the produce of the estate.

Further claims

Of shape built into line.

In Moscow as soon as he entered his huge house in which the faded and fading princesses still lived, with its enormous retinue; as soon as, driving through the town, he saw the Iberian shrine with innumerable tapers burning before the golden covers of the icons, the Kremlin Square with its snow undisturbed by vehicles, the sleigh drivers and hovels of the Sivtsev Vrazhok, those old Moscovites who desired nothing, hurried nowhere, and were ending their days leisurely; when he saw those old Moscow ladies, the Moscow balls, and the English Club, he felt himself at home in a quiet haven.

The spectator
hiding his uncertain springs.

It would be a mistake to think that this is ironic—a caricature of the historical accounts. On the contrary it is a very mild expression of the contradictory replies, not meeting the questions, which *all* the historians give, from the compilers of memoirs and the histories of separate states to the writers of general histories and the new histories of the *culture* of that period.

The story holding the man in.

"Yes, yes! I love him!" thought Natasha, reading the letter for the twentieth time and finding some peculiarly deep meaning in each word of it.

A series of
reductions.

"But every time there have been conquests there have been conquerors; every time there has been a revolution in any state there have been great men," says history. And, indeed, human reason replies: every time conquerors appear there have been wars, but this does not prove that the conquerors caused the wars and that it is possible to find the laws of a war in the personal activity of a single man. Whenever I look at my watch and its hands point to ten, I hear the bells of the neighboring church; but because the bells begin to ring when the hands of the clock reach ten, I have no right to assume that the movement of the bells is caused by the position of the hands of the watch.

Suppressed end

Where nothing is explained.

Next day the French army did not renew their attack, and the remnant of Bagration's detachnent was reunited to Kutuzov's army.

The town dissolves,
its factories work at night.

Rarely had Natasha experienced so joyful a feeling as now, sitting in the carriage beside the countess and gazing at the slowly receding walls of forsaken, agitated Moscow. Occasionally she leaned out of the carriage window and looked back and then forward at the long train of wounded in front of them. Almost at the head of the line she could see the raised hood of Prince Andrew's *calèche.* She did not know who was in it, but each time she looked at the procession her eyes sought that *calèche.* She knew it was right in front.

Signals in neutral terrain.

"We won't speak of it, my dear—I'll tell him everything; but one thing I beg of you, consider me your friend and if you want help, advice, or simply to open your heart to someone—not now, but when your mind is clearer—think of me!" He took her hand and kissed it. "I shall be happy if it's in my power..."

Fog explodes
into perfect control.

Natasha had married in the early spring of 1813, and in 1820 already had three daughters besides a son for whom she had longed and whom she was now nursing. She had grown stouter and broader, so that it was difficult to recognize in this robust, motherly woman the slim, lively Natasha of former days. Her features were more defined and had a calm, soft, and serene expression. In her face there was none of the ever-glowing animation that had formerly burned there and constituted its charm. Now her face and body were often all that one saw, and her soul was not visible at all.

A spasm of

Zig-zags of mannered sweeps.

Anatole with his swaggering air strode up to the window. He wanted to smash something. Pushing away the footmen he tugged at the frame, but could not move it. He smashed a pane.

The type of prose
departs in ascending steps.

"You did not get my letter?" he asked, and not waiting for a reply—which he would not have received, for the princess was unable to speak—he turned back, rapidly mounted the stairs again with the doctor who had entered the hall after him (they had met at the last post station), and again embraced his sister.

The perfectly natural figure's
tight orange face.

She was going straight on through the conservatory, neither seeing nor hearing anything, when suddenly the well-known whispering of Mademoiselle Bourienne aroused her. She raised her eyes, and two steps away saw Anatole embracing the Frenchwoman and whispering something to her. With a horrified expression on his handsome face, Anatole looked at Princess Mary, but did not at once take his arm from the waist of Mademoiselle Bourienne who had not yet seen her.

Exits take down signs.

As soon as the singing was over, another and another toast was proposed and Count Ilya Rostov became more and more moved, more glass was smashed, and the shouting grew louder. They drank to Bekleshëv, Naryshkin, Uvarov, Dolgorukov, Apraksin, Valuev, to the committee, to all the Club members and to all the Club guests, and finally to Count Ilya Rostov separately, as the organizer of the banquet. At that toast, the count took out his handkerchief and, covering his face, wept outright.

Obvious

Fragment.

The doctor glanced at his watch.

Wandering through
the static list.

During the first half of the journey—from Kremenchug to Kiev—all Rostov's thoughts, as is usual in such cases, were behind him, with the squadron; but when he had gone more than halfway he began to forget his three roans and Dozhoyveyko, his quartermaster, and to wonder anxiously how things would be at Otradnoe and what he would find there. Thoughts of home grew stronger the nearer he approached it—far stronger, as though this feeling of his was subject to the law by which the force of attraction is in inverse proportion to the square of the distance. At the last post station before Otradnoe he gave the driver a three-ruble tip, and on arriving he ran breathlessly, like a boy, up the steps of his home.

A fluorescent toy depicting a
miniature solar system.

Sonya and Natasha, in the light-blue dresses they had worn at the theater, looking pretty and conscious of it, were standing by the clavichord, happy and smiling. Vera was playing chess with Shinshin in the drawing room. The old countess, waiting for the return of her husband and son, sat playing patience with the old gentlewoman who lived in their house. Denisov, with sparkling eyes and ruffled hair, sat at the clavichord striking chords with his short fingers, his legs thrown back and his eyes rolling as he sang, with his small, husky, but true voice, some verses called "Enchantress," which he had composed, and to which he was trying to fit music:

*Enchantress, say, to my forsaken lyre*
*What magic power is this recalls me still?*
*What spark has set my inmost soul on fire,*
*What is this bliss that makes my fingers thrill?*

He was singing in passionate tones, gazing with his sparkling black-agate eyes at the frightened and happy Natasha.

Inert

metaphysic of

effect.

A very pretty curly-headed boy with a look of the Christ in the Sistine Madonna was depicted playing at stick and ball. The ball represented the terrestrial globe and the stick in his other hand a scepter.

At the same time

Everyone is aware of distance.

Pierre glanced round at the first cloud, which he had seen as a round compact ball, and in its place already were balloons of smoke floating to one side, and—"*puff*" (with a pause)—"*puff, puff*!" three and then four more appeared and then from each, with the same interval—"*boom—boom, boom*!" came the fine, firm, precise sounds in reply. It seemed as if those smoke clouds sometimes ran and sometimes stood still while woods, fields, and glittering bayonets ran past them. From the left, over fields and bushes, those large balls of smoke were continually appearing followed by their solemn reports, while nearer still, in the hollows and woods, there burst from the muskets small cloudlets that had no time to become balls, but had their little echoes in just the same way.

The irritant spins,
without any help from them.

When Anna Mikhaylovna returned from Count Bezukhov's the money, all in clean notes, was lying ready under a handkerchief on the countess' little table, and Anna Mikhaylovna noticed that something was agitating her.

A method to invent disbelief.

Sonya, shaking off some down which clung to her and tucking away the verses in the bosom of her dress close to her bony little chest, ran after Natasha down the passage into the sitting room with flushed face and light, joyous steps. At the visitors' request the young people sang the quartette, "The Brook," with which everyone was delighted. Then Nicholas sang a song he had just learned:

*At nighttime in the moon's fair glow*
*How sweet, as fancies wander free,*
*To feel that* in this world there's one
Who still is thinking but of thee!

No one decides
not to notice.

But on Tuesday evening, having come to Hélène's splendid salon, Boris received no clear explanation of why it had been necessary for him to come. There were other guests and the countess talked little to him, and only as he kissed her hand on taking leave said unexpectedly and in a whisper, with a strangely unsmiling face: "Come to dinner tomorrow... in the evening. You must come... Come!"

He would die

Resisting total thus achieved.

Absolute continuity of motion is not comprehensible to the human mind. Laws of motion of any kind become comprehensible to man only when he examines arbitrarily selected elements of that motion; but at the same time, a large proportion of human error comes from the arbitrary division of continuous motion into discontinuous elements. There is a well-known, so-called sophism of the ancients consisting in this, that Achilles could never catch up with a tortoise he was following, in spite of the fact that he traveled ten times as fast as the tortoise. By the time Achilles has covered the distance that separated him from the tortoise, the tortoise has covered one tenth of that distance ahead of him: when Achilles has covered that tenth, the tortoise has covered another one hundredth, and so on forever. This problem seemed to the ancients insoluble.

A record of
all that remains.

"One step beyond that boundary line which resembles the line dividing the living from the dead lies uncertainty, suffering, and death. And what is there? Who is there?—there beyond that field, that tree, that roof lit up by the sun? No one knows, but one wants to know. You fear and yet long to cross that line, and know that sooner or later it must be crossed and you will have to find out what is there, just as you will inevitably have to learn what lies the other side of death. But you are strong, healthy, cheerful, and excited, and are surrounded by other such excitedly animated and healthy men." So thinks, or at any rate feels, anyone who comes in sight of the enemy, and that feeling gives a particular glamour and glad keenness of impression to everything that takes place at such moments.

Museum tour
conducted by mutes.

Meanwhile, the city itself was deserted. There was hardly anyone in the streets. The gates and shops were all closed, only here and there round the taverns solitary shouts or drunken songs could be heard. Nobody drove through the streets and footsteps were rarely heard. The Povarskaya was quite still and deserted. The huge courtyard of the Rostovs' house was littered with wisps of hay and with dung from the horses, and not a soul was to be seen there.

Language
palpable as
continuum over shape.

We need only confess that we do not know the purpose of the European convulsions and that we know only the facts—that is, the murders, first in France, then in Italy, in Africa, in Prussia, in Austria, in Spain, and in Russia—and that the movements from the west to the east and from the east to the west form the essence and purpose of these events, and not only shall we have no need to see exceptional ability and genius in Napoleon and Alexander, but we shall be unable to consider them to be anything but like other men, and we shall not be obliged to have recourse to *chance* for an explanation of those small events which made these people what they were, but it will be clear that all those small events were inevitable.

"Substitute"

Not equal to stand for itself.

To the beekeeper's tap on the wall of the sick hive, instead of the former instant unanimous humming of tens of thousands of bees with their abdomens threateningly compressed, and producing by the rapid vibration of their wings an aerial living sound, the only reply is a disconnected buzzing from different parts of the deserted hive. From the alighting board, instead of the former spirituous fragrant smell of honey and venom, and the warm whiffs of crowded life, comes an odor of emptiness and decay mingling with the smell of honey. There are no longer sentinels sounding the alarm with their abdomens raised, and ready to die in defense of the hive. There is no longer the measured quiet sound of throbbing activity, like the sound of boiling water, but diverse discordant sounds of disorder.

Progress into
retreating barriers makes sense.

But not only was it impossible to make out what was happening from where he was standing down below, or from the knoll above on which some of his generals had taken their stand, but even from the *flèches* themselves—in which by this time there were now Russian and now French soldiers, alternately or together, dead, wounded, alive, frightened, or maddened—even at those *flèches* themselves it was impossible to make out what was taking place. There for several hours amid incessant cannon and musketry fire, now Russians were seen alone, now Frenchmen alone, now infantry, and now cavalry: they appeared, fired, fell, collided, not knowing what to do with one another, screamed, and ran back again.

Return to the beginning and note.

All these nobles, whom Pierre met every day at the Club or in their own houses, were in uniform—some in that of Catherine's day, others in that of the Emperor Paul, others again in the new uniforms of Alexander's time or the ordinary uniform of the nobility, and the general characteristic of being in uniform imparted something strange and fantastic to these diverse and familiar personalities, both old and young. The old men, dim-eyed, toothless, bald, sallow, and bloated, or gaunt and wrinkled, were especially striking. For the most part they sat quietly in their places and were silent, or, if they walked about and talked, attached themselves to someone younger.

Ends in a heap,<br>
exhausted.

At that instant the sun began to hide behind the clouds, and other stretchers came into view before Rostov. And the fear of death and of the stretchers, and love of the sun and of life, all merged into one feeling of sickening agitation.

Branches touch cloud

At the bottom of the well.

"If she goes to her cousin first and then to another lady, she will be my wife," said Prince Andrew to himself quite to his own surprise, as he watched her. She did go first to her cousin.

Print monitors<br>
illusion of depth.

Pierre had failed to notice Natasha because he did not at all expect to see her there, but he had failed to recognize her because the change in her since he last saw her was immense. She had grown thin and pale, but that was not what made her unrecognizable; she was unrecognizable at the moment he entered because on that face whose eyes had always shone with a suppressed smile of the joy of life, now when he first entered and glanced at her there was not the least shadow of a smile: only her eyes were kindly attentive and sadly interrogative.

Counter to
river stones, mineral samples.

One desperate, frightened yell from the first French soldier who saw the Cossacks, and all who were in the camp, undressed and only just waking up, ran off in all directions, abandoning cannons, muskets, and horses.

The moment of
mixed lots.

The colonel rode to the front, angrily gave some reply to questions put to him by the officers, and, like a man desperately insisting on having his own way, gave an order. No one said anything definite, but the rumor of an attack spread through the squadron. The command to form up rang out and the sabers whizzed as they were drawn from their scabbards. Still no one moved.

The skeleton at

The border instructs.

Before he reached him, Rostov, who was a splendid horseman, spurred Bedouin twice and successfully put him to the showy trot in which the animal went when excited. Bending his foaming muzzle to his chest, his tail extended, Bedouin, as if also conscious of the Emperor's eye upon him, passed splendidly, lifting his feet with a high and graceful action, as if flying through the air without touching the ground.

Spread

of the fingers

between keys.

Without looking at anyone, "Uncle" blew the dust off it and, tapping the case with his bony fingers, tuned the guitar and settled himself in his armchair. He took the guitar a little above the fingerboard, arching his left elbow with a somewhat theatrical gesture, and, with a wink at Anisya Fëdorovna, struck a single chord, pure and sonorous, and then quietly, smoothly, and confidently began playing in very slow time, not *My Lady*, but the well-known song: *Came a maiden down the street*. The tune, played with precision and in exact time, began to thrill in the hearts of Nicholas and Natasha, arousing in them the same kind of sober mirth as radiated from Anisya Fëdorovna's whole being. Anisya Fëdorovna flushed, and drawing her kerchief over her face went laughing out of the room.

Telephone poles

standing on disputed ground.

The combatants advanced along the trodden tracks, nearer and nearer to one another, beginning to see one another through the mist. They had the right to fire when they liked as they approached the barrier. Dolokhov walked slowly without raising his pistol, looking intently with his bright, sparkling blue eyes into his antagonist's face. His mouth wore its usual semblance of a smile.

The fountain gels.

Formerly, after he had given two or three orders and uttered a few phrases, marshals and adjutants had come galloping up with congratulations and happy faces, announcing the trophies taken, the corps of prisoners, bundles of enemy eagles and standards, cannon and stores, and Murat had only begged leave to loose the cavalry to gather in the baggage wagons. So it had been at Lodi, Marengo, Arcola, Jena, Austerlitz, Wagram, and so on. But now something strange was happening to his troops.

Blinks in the sun, intuitive

Technique.

Rostov submitted. He let the eight hundred remain and laid down a seven of hearts with a torn corner, which he had picked up from the floor. He well remembered that seven afterwards. He laid down the seven of hearts, on which with a broken bit of chalk he had written "800 rubles" in clear upright figures; he emptied the glass of warm champagne that was handed him, smiled at Dolokhov's words, and with a sinking heart, waiting for a seven to turn up, gazed at Dolokhov's hands which held the pack. Much depended on Rostov's winning or losing on that seven of hearts.

Rocks fill the eye
at the corners.

All eyes were gazing at her with one and the same expression. She could not fathom whether it was curiosity, devotion, gratitude, or apprehension and distrust—but the expression on all the faces was identical.

Sleeping man walks into house,
turns on the light.

"You've let the wolf go! . . . What sportsmen!" and as if scorning to say more to the frightened and shamefaced count, he lashed the heaving flanks of his sweating chestnut gelding with all the anger the count had aroused and flew off after the hounds. The count, like a punished schoolboy, looked round, trying by a smile to win Simon's sympathy for his plight. But Simon was no longer there. He was galloping round by the bushes while the field was coming up on both sides, all trying to head the wolf, but it vanished into the wood before they could do so.

Rolling
over hills to
concretize plains.

“You say you can’t see a reign of goodness and truth on earth. Nor could I, and it cannot be seen if one looks on our life here as the end of everything. On *earth*, here on this earth” (Pierre pointed to the fields), “there is no truth, all is false and evil; but in the universe, in the whole universe, there is a kingdom of truth, and we who are now the children of earth are—eternally—children of the whole universe. Don’t I feel in my soul that I am part of this vast harmonious whole? Don’t I feel that I form one link, one step, between the lower and higher beings, in this vast harmonious multitude of beings in whom the Deity—the Supreme Power if you prefer the term—is manifest?

“Because,

It can say that.”

“Something else is needed. When you stand expecting the overstrained string to snap at any moment, when everyone is expecting the inevitable catastrophe, as many as possible must join hands as closely as they can to withstand the calamity. Everything that is young and strong is being enticed away and depraved. One is lured by women, another by honors, a third by ambition or money, and they go over to that camp. No independent men, such as you or I, are left. What I say is widen the scope of our society, let the *mot d’ordre* be not virtue alone but independence and action as well!”

Threat of
motion from stills.

Sometimes he remembered how he had heard that soldiers in war when entrenched under the enemy’s fire, if they have nothing to do, try hard to find some occupation the more easily to bear the danger. To Pierre all men seemed like those soldiers, seeking refuge from life: some in ambition, some in cards, some in framing laws, some in women, some in toys, some in horses, some in politics, some in sport, some in wine, and some in governmental affairs. “Nothing is trivial, and nothing is important, it’s all the same—only to save oneself from it as best one can,” thought Pierre. “Only not to see *it*, that dreadful *it*!”

A statue surrounded by priests,
lying face down on the ground.

"How is it I am not moving? I have fallen, I am killed!" Rostov asked and answered at the same instant. He was alone in the middle of a field. Instead of the moving horses and hussars' backs, he saw nothing before him but the motionless earth and the stubble around him. There was warm blood under his arm. "No, I am wounded and the horse is killed." Rook tried to rise on his forelegs but fell back, pinning his rider's leg. Blood was flowing from his head; he struggled but could not rise. Rostov also tried to rise but fell back, his sabretache having become entangled in the saddle. Where our men were, and where the French, he did not know. There was no one near.

A puffy rope,
gathered manfully.

Five minutes later, Denisov came into the hut, climbed with muddy boots on the bed, lit his pipe, furiously scattered his things about, took his leaded whip, buckled on his saber, and went out again. In answer to Rostov's inquiry where he was going, he answered vaguely and crossly that he had some business.

Wish for

Invulnerable sentence, walking
in air.

"And yet what a splendid reign your master *might have had*!"

Thought
mechanics of emphasis places in
reach.

The princess glanced at her watch and, seeing that she was five minutes late in starting her practice on the clavichord, went into the sitting room with a look of alarm. Between twelve and two o'clock, as the day was mapped out, the prince rested and the princess played the clavichord.

Decapitated mannequin
takes a few steps.

Pierre gazed now with dazed eyes at these sharpshooters who ran in couples out of the circle. All but one rejoined their companies. This one, a young soldier, his face deadly pale, his shako pushed back, and his musket resting on the ground, still stood near the pit at the spot from which he had fired. He swayed like a drunken man, taking some steps forward and back to save himself from falling.

Inherent strain.

Glinka, the editor of the *Russian Messenger*, who was recognized (cries of "author! author!" were heard in the crowd), said that "hell must be repulsed by hell," and that he had seen a child smiling at lightning flashes and thunderclaps, but "we will not be that child."

Unlocatable

Entrance at odds with address.

"*Und die ganze Welt hoch* [And hurrah for the whole world]!"

Window glass
obscures the intended effect.

At the edge of the road stood an oak. Probably ten times the age of the birches that formed the forest, it was ten times as thick and twice as tall as they. It was an enormous tree, its girth twice as great as a man could embrace, and evidently long ago some of its branches had been broken off and its bark scarred. With its huge ungainly limbs sprawling unsymmetrically, and its gnarled hands and fingers, it stood an aged, stern, and scornful monster among the smiling birch trees. Only the dead-looking evergreen firs dotted about in the forest, and this oak, refused to yield to the charm of spring or notice either the spring or the sunshine.

Ventilation furnished with keys.

But on the eighth of August a committee, consisting of Field Marshall Saltykov, Arakcheev, Vyazmitinov, Lopukhin, and Kochubey met to consider the progress of the war. This committee came to the conclusion that our failures were due to a want of unity in the command and though the members of the committee were aware of the Emperor's dislike of Kutuzov, after a short deliberation they agreed to advise his appointment as commander in chief. That same day Kutuzov was appointed commander in chief with full powers over the armies and over the whole region occupied by them.

Thereafter fused,
heated to an improbable degree.

Princess Mary pressed his hand. The pressure made him wince just perceptibly. He was silent, and she did not know what to say. She now understood what had happened to him two days before. In his words, his tone, and especially in that calm, almost antagonistic look could be felt an estrangement from everything belonging to this world, terrible in one who is alive. Evidently only with an effort did he understand anything living; but it was obvious that he failed to understand, not because he lacked the power to do so but because he understood something else—something the living did not and could not understand—and which wholly occupied his mind.

*for Ron Silliman*

# Question of Interpretation

## I

Because they continue in some manner
To project that element of wishful fantasy
We call love—regardless, and unconcerned,
Even if, or likely as, there is no consequence.

## II

The choked chord overarching the road
Noise they call "realia." Even this writing.
We/you/I/they/she/it presents evidence.
Now I am looking back. (Don't answer.)

## III

Sans voice in a cloud of devious meanings
You wrap around any concrete object only
To interpret it endlessly, preying on the deficit
Left behind from their inexact posturings.

## IV

In Freud's great parable, the *fort/da*
The spindle goes round, it goes round.
The confusion is all in the absence
And the pleasure in the observation.

### V

See, they return—to a point of departure
They had never known, for a moment.
Leaning backwards over a railing while
We stare at each other, upside down.

### VI

Oceanic feelings at the shoreline
Of memory trees in the mountains.
These were parts of our condition
Before we knew how to speak it.

### VII

Trust me, please—absolutely
Until errancy is all message.
A question deserves an answer
But gets answered nonetheless.

### VIII

These are our feelings. There they are.
Behind them, a line of cars waiting
Behind a double row of semi trailers
Loaded with cargo for El Dorado.

## IX

What is belief? If there is no question
Of motivation, there cannot be a belief.
We comprehend what we can grasp but
Only ironically, on stage, in performance.

## X

Like a river flowing down concrete steps
Pleasure is splitting into several streams
Of being overwhelmed and flooded, the
Waters subsiding as we are carried down.

## XI

This must be desire for something
That is not there—"irrealia." Back of
The head, while staring directly forward.
For one week only, and then—one day.

## XII

If only for a millionth of a second
Or less, brighter than anything—
It is I being extinguished, coronal.
Knowledge at the core. It is not I.

*in memory of Martin Watten*

## Blue States
(After Fearing)

*paint the town blue*

Yes, you
everywhere you, driving, laughing, arranging the day†

MARILYN MONROE FOUND ALIVE, the headline on the tabloid read. Most disturbing was the picture: depressed face over age-advanced body. Years later, nothing left of the ideal.

Champagne for supper, murder for breakfast, romance
for lunch and terror for tea

To be subject in the era we are in is to be defined by a series of defeats and still maintain one's position. All else is simply the construction of norms, means/ends rationality.

Adjust to the present, and to a longer view.
To cities shining in the sky tonight, and smoking in the
dust tomorrow

In what sense is 51% a mandate? When capital accumulates by such margins of profit. "I earned political capital, and now I intend to spend it." Thus 1.5% represents the general will.

No name, any name, nowhere, nothing, no one, none

I am a pixel on an enormous screen; my words have no effect—I am a unit, an isolated person standing in a long line to vote, separated from all the others, waiting to be counted.

They do not hear each other now—
They listen to voices in themselves
Mad with perfect sanity

An outlier poll at 5 P.M. Election Day showed 311 electoral votes Blue and Virginia and Nevada in doubt. This is *not* now a matter of record—it was removed from their site.

then the news: somewhere a million men are on the
march again, elsewhere the horror mounts

What is the mechanism of fear? The terrorist tape, reasonable men agree, did not affect the election. It did not, in any reasonable way—but it may have been a visceral trigger.

Here we will be urged by reality confused with dream.
We will be urged by the hunger of the live, invited by
the relentless purposes of millions

The answer to the political debacle of the present is to return to a politics of the Popular Front, its antifascism. It is *not* a matter of coalition; we need something to be *against*.

She thought it was too soon but they said no, it was
too late. They didn't trust the other people

Should I have taught Robert Glück's novel *Margery Kempe* a week before the election? Did it confuse the students, give them nothing to stand on? This was my thought.

Knowing that the bartender, and the elk's head, and the
picture of some forgotten champion...
Must somehow be aware of us, too

What would be signs of fascism creeping into the subjectivity of the state? Two kinds of evidence: destructive expansion of national fantasy; radical scapegoating of intolerable others.

scenes, hysterics, peace
live, live, live, live, and then move out

Are we depressed yet? Should we emigrate to Canada? Take a few years off and live in poetic exile? What is the most immediate and available form of adaptive behavior?

With who the hell are you at the corner of his casket,
and where the hell we going on the right-hand
silver knob

This rhetoric of aggression is a condition of public agency. But the conduct of the election as an aggressive debate turned out to be an enormous risk—as aggressivity turned to rage.

Now listen, wait, will you listen for a minute? That's all
I ask. Yes or no?

The moment of intervention passes as it is caught in retrospection of the unfolding story we are in. The most damaging part of the election was the triumphalism of the day after.

That popular ghost, Franklin Devoe, serial hero of the
current magazines,
the exact, composite dream of those who read

One can go to bed thinking the world is one thing and wake up convinced it is another. And everyone will act in such a way as to confirm this view, even if nothing has changed.

Is the night that wraps all the huts of the south and folds
the empty barns of the west;
is the wind that fans the roadside fire

I am happy to be living in a Blue state. In Blue states, there is a chance of a meaningful politics. Blue states remember the history that created them. Blue states are critical.

The crime, if there was a crime, has not been reported
as yet;
The plot, if that is what it was, is still a secret

I await news of the manipulations that took place behind the scenes—the computer chip in voting machines, the trashing of registrations, denial on basis of race. But it won't matter.

Hand in hand, heart joined to heart,
A new day dawned,
Happy and sweet and sunny and pure

The nothing that exploded, exploded in more than one way. The fantasy that is everywhere began as a mere nothing, while a fantasy of what will be has now disappeared.

With 2,000 wounded and 1,000 dead
10,000 wounded and 5,000 dead
100,000 wounded and 50,000 dead

The numbers are automatic, insubstantial. They exist as a negative—vanishing into abstraction, crushing in their weight. We are only ourselves as part of the whole.

Would you like to live, yourself, the way that other people do
would you like to be the kind of man you've always
dreamed you'd be

This writing may be beneficial for me, but there is no guarantee it is for you. Maybe you will take back the power they took from you—but individually, on a competing basis.

Lady, the demand is for a dream that lives and grows
and does not fade when the midnight theater
special pulls out on track 15

If you were not part of my dream, I would do to you what you would do to me, if I were not part of yours. The results are inconclusive, and there are no words to report them.

And we will fight for all of this again, and if need be again,
And on that day, and in that place, we will try again, and
this time we shall win

You desperately need a win. So do I—if I don't win again soon, I will lapse into nonentity. We rush to where there can be a win, flee from anywhere we fail to come out on top.

This key responds with something not even sound at all,
sometimes a feeling, and the feeling is anguish

The key is the displaced counter of human contact. Eyes avert from those whose thoughts do not coincide with mine. A process of asociality sets in, appearing to be inevitable.

THE TWENTIETH CENTURY COMES BUT ONCE

once too soon, and just a little too fast

The disaster is an afterimage of a hurricane passing up the I-4 corridor, sweeping everything before it in a monumental fear. Operatives channel this fear, direct it to their ends.

Of the indubitable beginning of life, and of its indubitable
end,
Of the mirage within a mirage

Belated I began, belatedly I will end. The twentieth century ended too; we are in another era, where prior results are revised. "The only thing I know is to wipe the slate clean…"

"Hi-Fi Sue Scores Again,"
"*Think!* names this average, all-round girl America's
sweetheart of the year"—

In what way can a complex be undone? It's simple, stupid. The Gordian Knot is the parable most loved by the Right. All analysis flies in the face of a simple, stupid act.

For it is the end, surely? We knew the story to be
working toward an end, and this, then, is in fact
the end?

The routes are prefigured in advance. We lay down networks of reinforced concrete between identification points, and it all works perfectly, toward a predetermined goal.

Writing must be such a nice profession.

Fill in the coupon. How do you know? Maybe you can be

a writer, too

Afraid of depression, they reproduce it. Evidently, they are happy with the results. In desperate times, the poet represents the general will, beyond the fact of presidents.

nothing unto you, and nothing unto me, or to
any other known or unknown party or parties,
living or deceased

He was a monad in a chartered space, sealed off from fluctuation; he owned the market; he was the rock on which our hopes and fears were founded, the last to be liquidated.

Does he think that he is the only one?
Does he think that he is the only man on earth who has
felt this thing?

Joining together in massive numbers, they rose up, expressing a will that had been suppressed until that moment—to find their numbers fell short. In this they were confirmed.

It is destiny that is yours, yours, all yours, and only yours,
a fate you have long ago disowned and disavowed

What a ridiculous fantasy, that merely to reach out and touch each other we could reinvent the world that was taken away. That we could end *ressentiment*, could think otherwise.

Then the doorbell rings. Then Peg drops in. And Bill.
And Jane. And Doc.

Could it be otherwise? At the theaters, the people stand in line,
forgetting what could have been—only to confirm it as the
general will. This entertainment was made for them.

There is no law compelling any man on earth to do the
same, second hand.
I am tired of following invisible lives down intangible
avenues to fathomless ends

In the dream, a female lion with delicate face, elongated limbs, and
matted fur emerged from woods by the side of the road. We were
merely driving by in our car, windows rolled up.

Then enter again, through a strange door, into a life
again all strange,
Enter as a rich man, or perhaps a poor man

"The perfectibility of man" appears as a ghostly afterimage down
a long corridor where he thinks he sees a version of himself,
walking forward to that moment in which he was.

The telephone is gone, the phone that rang and rang,
and never did connect with any other phone,
And the great steel safe where no diamonds ever were—

The condition of evaporating as a narrative of progress—we are
everywhere, all at once, while in truth we are disappearing.
A condition of precipitation is the poetics of truth.

The actual voice, or this muted thunder? These giant
shadows, or the naked face?
Or something within the voice or behind the face?

I do not consent to the situation we are in. I do not consent to the war, to the farce of consent staged to permit it. The voice that speaks is thus subtracted from a face.

Would you care to bring in the stations past the stars
would you care to tune in on your dead love's grave?

At the exact moment of lunar eclipse, the Red Sox win the Series. An impossible event is uninterpretable. We dare not interpret it as meaning anything, one way or the other.

But what it if is, what if it is, what if it is, what if the thing
that cannot happen really happens just the same

Floating from anxiety, lifting from fear. The impossible event ends uncertainty—so that we can say, with all the rest, that we witnessed what took place, if from a peculiar perspective.

but how will you know us, crumbled into ashes, lost in
air and water and fire and stone
how will you know us, now or at any time

Weeks later, the time drifts, we refuse information, snow falls, bodies pile up, the time drifts, they are using us, we refuse information, there are the bodies, snow falls, information.

Not the saga of your soul at grips with fate,
bleedingheart, for we have troubles of our own

They pulled the message once it became outdated. A billboard reading "Who cares?" replaced by a solicitation for hospital services: "We do." The public face had disappeared.

A few of them, sometimes, choose record number 9,
Or sometimes number 12,
And once in a while someone likes selection 5

The number 43 is up. Empty equivalents of capital replace a universal. We rage in our particularity against the blinding illumination of a uniform sky. The number 6 is up.

Movies at night: "The life she led."
Everyone sleeps in one big bed

Dreams divide into heavy traffic in extreme weather. Dan Rather signs off from the nightly news; substitution and overwriting are the face of John Roberts. There is nothing to report.

That as long as you wish you may see these streets and
        parks with the same eyes,
The same mood as today—

Logic and fiction conjoin in a univocal effect. The index of belief rises, unbelievably! I refuse to accept any evidence of an outcome, even as every outcome is deferred.

And it comes to this: That always I feel another hand,
        not mine, has drawn and turned the card to find
        some incredible ace

They will take a baseball bat to your wounded mattress, hurl a bowling ball into your metal firewall, spray toxic solvents onto your painted forehead, poison your impulse to resist.

If they catch you, it is said, they make you rap, rap, rap
        on a table all night,

And blow through a trumpet and float around the room
in long white veils

Inflation spirals upward through devaluing trends. The imported cheese is a loss leader. Our numbers add up, incalculable. Notice posted on the front door: "I accept / do not accept."

Name, address, relatives, religion, income, sex, bank
account, insurance, health, race, experience, age

Alberta touches Saskatchewan, Saskatchewan senses Manitoba, Manitoba leans on Ontario, Ontario embraces Quebec. We lie breathlessly with trading partners in the night.

These are the things that will return to you,
to mingle vividly with the days and nights, with the
sound of motors and the sun's warmth

There is trouble with your account. New information is requested. Do not reply to this message; it has been sent by an alien proxy. You will not be given another chance to reply.

WHO, WHO, WHO?
WHAT WERE YOU WHEN, WHY WERE YOU WHAT, WHERE WERE
YOU WHICH, EITHER HOW OR WHY?

Sun melts snow on black asphalt, leaving the road clear for drivers. All necessary products have been supplied, the maintenance contracts signed, sealed, and delivered.

Because the mind is a common sense affair filled with
common sense answers to common sense facts,
It can add up, can add up, can add up, can add up

Another word I did not write appears in the spirit parchment prepared
by me. The security firm does not know the contents of the trunk,
but it will be delivered just the same.

(Oh happy divorce)
(But you'd better not say that. Think of the relatives. And
the public, by and large, would not believe you

Signs pass in succession along the road to the airport. People are
galvanized for a change in government. One aircraft after another
taxis onto the runway. People assemble.

Now don't get excited. We'll just keep quiet and deal
the cards and whoever it is they'll get tired and
go away. How many for you?

If there is to be movement, it must be in a single direction. Around
the shrinking icecap, magnetic attractions discharge their fields.
People rise up to change their government.

so write it out on a bill-board that stands
under the yellow light of an "L" platform
among popcorn wrappers and cigarette butts

People rise up and change your government! Snow falls, to be cleared
away by machines. The archive is accessible but contains no
entries. This is the *sensus communis*, I repeat.

*in memory of Bill Berkson*

## Zone
## (Correlation)

> Why even speak of "I," he dreams,
> which interests me almost not at all?
>
> —William Carlos Williams, *Paterson*

### I

> In regard to the poems I left with you; will you
> be so kind as to return them to me at my new
> address?‡

Communication proceeds apace, regardless the
missed encounter. The poem you did not read is
information, a lack of reading become knowledge.
Acknowledgment is the necessary complement
to knowledge, apart from which the poem is mere
information. The poem, which you did not read, is
(disavowed) my own, my own best self, who I am.

### II

> I have said that the artist is an Ishmael; Call
> me Ishmael, says Melville in the very first line
> of Moby Dick; he is the wild ass of a man;—
> Ishmael means affliction.

Our intentions wildly miss the point, of necessity.
The poet is one who tolerates the missed encounter
and ends up writing of it—overcoming disconnection.

III

and
a photograph-holder with pictures of himself
between the two children, all returned
weeping, weeping—

The placeholder of the human is our loss of self, figured in terms of another. We go out of our minds looking for a lost memento of presence to ourselves, as we were known to another. In the space between another and ourselves, something has gone missing. We go out of our minds to replace and preserve it.

IV

Excursions came from great distances in the
United States and even from Canada to see
the wonder.

The distance to a sublime event unites the people and brings them together. Hence prodigies, wonders, miracles, capacious views, dynamic eruptions, freaks of nature, disasters, earthquakes, hurricanes—allow them to find a common place in awe of that which exceeds them. Communication is incommensurate.

V

but apart, observant of
the distress, sweeps down or up clearing
the spray—

brings in the rumors of separate
worlds

Mind's closed captioning tracks the ineffable vision
and assigns values to it, which emerge into knowing.
But these forms have never been here before, hence
the rumors of the great and strange from which they
must have been sent forth. Mind can only understand
what mind presents to itself in a form of processing
that which has originated from entirely elsewhere.

VI

> He has never been able to sit up, as he cannot support the enormous weight of his head; but he is constantly in a large cradle, with his head supported on pillows.

Mind becomes unwieldy until it accedes to body;
quality devolves into quantity, springs forth again.

VII

> keeping nevertheless to the stream, they
> retake their course, the air full
> of the tumult and of spray
> connotative of the equal air, coeval,
> filling the void

Bits streaming forward over bandwidth create a frame
for cognitive mapping in surges that do not cease by
reason of interruption but modularly press forward.

VIII

> Refused
> she shrank within herself. She too refused.

Even as the event of a missed encounter takes on
the attributes of a completed act of communication.

IX

> Boys in bathing had often reported the bottom
> as full of big snakes that had touched their feet
> and limbs but they were without doubt the eels.

Content, trope of the most familiar, most estranged.
Philosophers cast their nets but it is the random and
contingent throw that brings the undisclosed content
into the light. These thoughts are indescribably base,
but we knew they were at bottom all along, certainly!

X

> And derivatively, for the Great Falls,
> PISS-AGH! the giant lets fly!

Second-order discourse is the song of the great,
predicated on the distance from greatness to small.
The people sing the song of the great as overflowing
greatness into the pool of their being, and it flows.
Second-order discourse becomes our primary song.

XI

> I found her in bed. However, she had helped
> "Billy" do up the work. My mother has always
> tried to do her part, and she is always trying to
> do something for her children.

Connate to the mind of the native is thought as a structure of shared reality—affirmed in the telling, but latent nonetheless. Each fragment they utter unfolds the world in which communication makes sense. Language is a theory of the people, without which they would be aimless and without direction. Language organizes the people in their unthinking.

XII

And the myth
that holds up the rock,
that holds up the water thrives there—
in that cavern, that profound cleft

In being the most terrible authority on earth, matter splits us from our place within it. Matter makes void the substance of our relation, that has no substance. Therefore we search out voids and incommensurates in order to chart the record of our loss. Everything we say echoes with its fundamental, missing substrate.

XIII

where the deer run
and the wood-duck nests protecting his
gallant plumage

Sensed immediacy is supported by a substrate of dream as the matrix all figures of mind are cast in.

XIV

> The twaalft, or striped bass was also abundant,
> and even sturgeon, of a huge bigness, were
> frequently caught:—

Producing content beyond our understanding of it, each eruption is dated to a particular time and place.

XV

> (Thence Carlos had fled in the 70's
> leaving the portraits of my grandparents,
> the furniture, the silver, even the meal
> hot upon the table before the Revolutionists
> coming in at the far end of the street.)

At the end of a protocol of questioning the world there is a constructed scene that mimics the whole into which we are being drawn. Our revolution will be to bring the whole into the present as its missing double, a ghost affect we carry with us at all times.

XVI

> Grapes in April, orchids
> like weeds, uncut, at tropic
> heat while the snow flies, left
> to droop on the stem, not even
> exhibited at the city show.

Democracy is parataxis, aristocracy hypotaxis. As forms of organization, neither can exist without the other. In a democracy, the artist establishes her rule.

XVII

> News of this sale created such excitement that search for the pearls was started throughout the country. The Unios (mussels) at Notch Brook and elsewhere were gathered by the millions and destroyed often with little or no result.

Quality accedes to quantity as a pearl of great price
sets the terms for value that are generally accepted.
Likewise with the artist, whose made thing of unique
quality becomes a measure by which all value is set.
The artist establishes a rule and then comments on
its deficient application—casting pearls before swine
as much as to say, by these tokens may you know
the depth to which your bereft quantity has fallen,
and with that establish a measure to trade on it!

XVIII

> Inside the bus one sees
> his thoughts sitting and standing. His
> thoughts alight and scatter—

Algorithms of uniqueness and recurrence combine to
produce phenomena we experience in everyday life.
Such delusional thoughts are the inflamed residue of
our mere calculations, so that calculating machines
reproduce their order in our perception of the world.
We reject the sum total, which is always prefigured,
while we watch in fascination as the numbers add up.
Numbered players leap under the lights, lighter than
air, fading away into their shot, which arcs and hits.
We experience a thrill when the number increases.

XIX

with the roar of the river
forever in our ears (arrears)
inducing sleep and silence, the roar
of eternal sleep . .

The roar of machine noise as traffic bursts through gates of concrete channels and onward in measured increments of flow that wax and wane from 0 to 1.

XX

It is the ignorant sun
rising in the slot of
hollow suns risen, so that never in this
world will a man live well in his body
save dying—

The recurrence of that burst of energy we call sun on a daily basis, and the decline of its heat and light, are the measure by which we think to know but cannot imagine the form of our unknowing in its recurrence.

XXI

A quart of potatoes, half a dozen oranges,
a bunch of beets and some soup greens.
Look, I have a new set of teeth. Why you
look ten years younger .

In democratic form, content seeks its own level by the force of its displacement from the absent norm which it is in the process of creating. Absence then defines the facticity of the content creating norms. The positive is that impossible but dumbly insisted upon in a series that ratifies itself as only possible. These things that you have made sensible for us, are they the materials of poetry? The poetry is just these things; the poetry is a displacement that can be enacted only where such things will never be.

XXII

> Twice a month Paterson receives
> communications from the Pope and Jacques
> Barzun
> (Isocrates). His works
> have been done into French
> and Portuguese.

Coming in, going out—centrifugal, centripetal—information locates the common center that unites sender and receiver in the throughput of dispersal. This is a knowledge sentence that attempts to say what a complex form of activity really is and does. Thus it takes the form of a complex, but differently.

XXIII

> There were in 1870, native born 20,711, which
> would of course include children of foreign
> parents; foreign 12,868 of whom 237 were French,
> 1,420 German, 3,343 English—(Mr. Lambert who
> later built the Castle among them), 5,124 Irish,
> 879 Scotch, 1,360 Hollanders and 170 Swiss—

Homogeneity leads from dispersal, heterogeneity from consolidation—and back and forth again. The native-born son is pressed by circumstances to leave the home, encountering the foreign-born moving in. A native can only be a state of desire leading from stasis to mobility and given his nature thereby, while a foreigner seeks her limit so as to be known as fixity defined throughout her movement. And a territory is the ground created at the boundary of the two.

## XXIV

> This was the starting point of Sam Patch's career as a famous jumper. I saw that, said the old man with satisfaction, and I don't believe there is another person in town today who was an eye-witness of that scene.

A unique event defines him through all duration, but as he repeated the event a million times, his identity was dispersed, rejoining the stream of inchoate flux. Out of the bitstream an electrical surge flooded the channel, eradicating the message, and exploding the terminal—an event not describable within the system.

## XXV

> Eternally asleep,
> his dreams walk about the city where he
> persists incognito.

Fitfully awake, we see into the depths of structure.

XXVI

The horse, the bull
the whole din of fracturing thought
as it falls tinnily to nothing upon the streets
and the absurd dignity of a locomotive
hauling freight—

Here is that discontinuity of image with language as the source of language's most pronounced effects. Sound clatters in the register of defunct replication likewise. Therefore, behold man—*ecce homo*—in all his puny efforts at correspondence and causality, the linking of one discontinuous moment with the next.

XXVII

The rose is green and will bloom,
overtopping you, green, livid
green when you shall no more speak, or
taste, or even be

Broken up, the message given forth by nature roars in spaces where there are no antennae to pick it up. Caverns underneath the sea, polar ice caps, depths of tropical forests, endless plains of desert landscapes where there is no one—offer us primary evidence.

XXVIII

Around the falling waters the Furies hurl!
Violence gathers, spins in their heads
summoning them:

Scale overwhelms a solitary reaper returning to her hut beside the busy motorway leading to a major city. Speed passes by the single figure armed with gauges to record a mechanical movement from point A to B. Tripwires by the path, electrical warning devices, and motion detectors alert researchers to the presence of the species. En route from the high forest, the animal gives no warning of its arrival, leaves no trace of its departure. Books have been written about its habits.

## XXIX

Ain't they beautiful?

Definition of the great is the avowal of emphasis as that form of sociality implied by a judgment of taste. As it is incommunicable, we can only communicate it in a form of empty affirmation, bald approximation, lucid expostulation, a *cri de coeur* without substance, foaming at the mouth, eruption of animal madness. Each enunciation takes its place in the verbal order.

## XXX

the river comes pouring in above the city
and crashes from the edge of the gorge
in a recoil of spray and rainbow mists—

At increased volume, the roar became personified as the singular, unifying voice that had been held back in abeyance. He needs the roar in his head so as to make individual words be discrete and perceptible. Detaching from the mass of sonic substrate, word follows word, leading on to articulated structures—structures that were there all along, if inaccessible.

## XXXI

The melting snow
dripped from the cornice by his window
90 strokes a minute—

Words attach to a palpable blankness which, had it not been named, would have been identical to itself. Words introject a foreign element into all sameness.

## XXXII

*in distinctive terms; by multiplication a*
*reduction to one; daring; a fall; the clouds resolved*
*into a sandy sluice; an enforced pause*

I understand the necessity here: it is to disclose the position of the author, distribute it among materials. The authorship resulting will only be the more grand, its risks bordering on the sublime. Let us, therefore, refigure all authorship as a form of displacement that we might take up the task of reinventing the world. Solidarity in unlikeness forever, with a world to win!

## XXXIII

The language, the language
fails them
They do not know the words
or have not
the courage to use them .

You who are at rest cannot comprehend movement.

XXXIV

I. Leadership passes into empire; empire begets insolence; insolence brings ruin.

Those who risk only movement make a fatal error: there is no second-order comprehension for them.

XXXV

The theme
is as it may prove: asleep, unrecognized—
all of a piece, alone
in a wind that does not move the others—

Writing provides an inevitable dissociation of order. In regular lines, writing unlinks all that it aligns, with the only proviso being that one thing follow another. The act of writing itself declares a period of time, just as any other period of time is declared. But not any period of time, once declared, may be set forth in writing. It both does and does not record the day.

XXXVI

(What common language to unravel?

The horizon of language unfolds from the complexity in which we are embedded. But on whose authority does it so unfold? He who first decided to exit from it, to find an alternative to our complexity in language.

Thus standing outside, he tries to order its complexity along the lines of his decision to do so. In so doing, he declares the properties of a language that is not natural. Here, I offer you one brick—take it as a word, as the basis for a language of 800 bricks. Every error follows error, to construct a new language of bricks.

## XXXVII

> It must have been varnished over, he argued, to have it stick that way. One corner of it he'd got loose in spite of all and would get the rest presently: talking pleasantly the while and with great skill to the anxious parent.

A word whose label is stuck to the thing—definition of useless. Only by getting it unstuck will we ever have a chance to reattach it, but that would only lead us to much useless and unwarranted labor. Thus language ought to be understood as conventional, it turns out.

## XXXVIII

> He shifts his change:

The ground on which he seeks to found his empire: an unstable ground of language that is incapable of representing a thing. Language thereby splits into a productively unstable ground, always issuing forth, a chasm between one uncertain state and another. Breaks in continuity are a compelling distress that issues forth an illusion of continuity to begin with. He is immersed in the plenitude surrounding him, compelled to break with it nonetheless to escape.

## XXXIX

The water pouring still
from the edge of the rocks, filling
his ears with its sound, hard to interpret.

Between infrastructure and information, sound of machine transport on a bitstream highway ascends, filling space and time with an indescribable roaring that conveys material and immaterial content to its desired ends. Forks in the road add to nodal points along a decision tree that specifies where content is in time and space, as well as its likelihood of delivery. Information locating this content is thus of high value, even as the infrastructure delivers goods regardless of quality—the greatest goods for the greatest number.

## XL

"The 7th, December, this year, (1737) at night,
was a large shock of an earthquake, accompanied
with a remarkable rumbling noise; people waked
in their beds, the doors flew open, bricks fell
from the chimneys; the consternation was
serious, but happily no great damage ensued."

The great awakening could come from anywhere, at any time, but it only takes place in precise historical circumstances. It is just so with the interruption of our understanding as a necessity for all understanding—for which we assign it a time and give it a date. The poem is a record of this kind of happening. Therefore, the poem is datable and the form of a unique event.

Even at the intersection of the information highway,
where content is distributed as if a common good,
the poem happens only once in the way it does.

XLI

Innumerable women, each like a flower.

But

only one man—like a city.

If the nature of each one is their freedom, then each must be alone. Nature, like the other, is of high-value information, demanding specificity. Only in a city can each find a generality conducive to life. As inspecific, a city is background noise for the nature it produces.

XLII

On peering intently at times as the torrent sank and rose, he could distinctly see the legs of a man, the body being lodged between the two logs, in a very extraordinary manner. It was in the "crotch" of these logs that the body was caught.

Nature drags inspecific man toward time and place.

XLIII

Into the sewer they threw the dead horse.
What birth does this foretell? I think
he'll write a novel bye and bye .

Nature made the inspecific generality of the city into high-value information—thus ending its form of life as various and multiple, tying it to a unique outcome.

XLIV

New Barbadoes Neck, the region was called.
Cromwell, in the middle of the seventeenth
century, shipped some thousands of Irish women
and children to the Barbadoes to be sold as slaves.

Against all natural determination, hybridity emerges as the only alternative. Hybrid forms of life give back to the city its mixed, inspecific, undisclosed quality. The multitude is renewed in its low-value quantity.

XLV

certainly NOT the university,
a green bud fallen upon the pavement its
sweet breath suppressed: Divorce (the
language stutters)

As the high-value information of nature falls, so the certainty of low-value knowledge rises. A knowledge of commonality is the only knowledge available, until it becomes restricted, intractable, unavailable for use. Nature is always an incursion on the commonality of the multitude. Thus the crowds on weekends—at seashores, mountain trails, and parks—reflect on it. Death becomes a national park, crowded on week-ends with self-reflexive, unconscious nature lovers.

XLVI

What
irritation of offensively red brick is this,
red as poor-man's flesh? Anachronistic?
The mystery
of streets and back rooms—

Death invests a university of high-value knowledge.
The people do not accede to the university until the
knowledge they brought with them is ready to die.

XLVII

—Say it, no ideas but in things—
nothing but the blank faces of the houses
and cylindrical trees

The particular does not accede to the universal
until it be an accident that declares substance.

XLVIII

erect, a proud queen, conscious of her power,
mud-caked, her monumental hair
slanted above the brows—violently frowning

As any substance seeks to eliminate its accident.

XLIX

making an impossible moat between the high
and the low where

the life once flourished . . knowledge
of the avenues of information—

This sentence is tripartite, divided according to rule. Everyone, we agree, knows what it means to say *is. Is* is at the basis of this sentence to compel agreement.

L

Mr. and Mrs. Cummings walked over the solid ledge to the vicinity of the cataract, charmed with the wonderful prospect, and making various remarks about the stupendous works of nature around them.

Information is the metapoetics of knowledge. Their fatal error—to be drawn by the lure of the sublime—was only half of their misunderstanding. The people are saturated with the discourse of their multiplicity until, lured deathward, they begin to understand it.

LI

A history that has, by its den in the
rocks, bole and fangs, its own cane-brake
whence, half hid, canes and stripes
blending, it grins (beauty defied)

Democracy is impossible, and it must be preserved. For us, democracy has become a belief in what can not emerge—until it does and the basis for our belief returns. I declare the end of democracy—a speech made to preserve democracy and intensify belief.

## LII

A false language. A true. A false language
pouring—a language (misunderstood) pouring
(misinterpreted) without dignity, without
minister, crashing upon a stone ear.

Death rides the waves of entertainment to become
famous. And so the people say, "famous as death."
Once dead, one can only become as famous as death.
There is no development in these thoughts, only stasis.
Poetry is the thought that conveys no development—
only a break between one thing and the next. The
people think the little death is what will make them
famous. Dying, we break into things that last forever.

## LIII

N. F. PATERSON
(N for Noah; F for Faitoute; P for short)
"Jersey Lightning" to the boys.

On information and the rights of man (outside view):
the overview of all the days gave them a conceptual
framework through which all things appear minute
and unimportant. Details are their undoing, lost as
they are within them, without any hope of escape.
On knowledge and the rights of man (inside view):
they framed their understanding in the proper way,
proceeding from one thing to the next, enlightened.

LIV

> "Rigor of beauty is the quest. But how will you find beauty when it is locked in the mind past all remonstrance?"

What does it mean to write a knowledge sentence? This question conveys all it can legitimately contain, even as its information is locked up in the sentence. Only by opening up the implicit frames by which our knowledge is contained might we gain access to it. Each word in succession is an index to a frame that locks away knowledge it contains. Open the frames—by which to convey the door, the house, the city!

LV

> We sit and talk, sensing a little
> the rushing impact of the giants'
> violent torrent rolling over us

It is outside, the ground of a language equal to our desire. For our desire is to be outside any order that contains us, the frame we carry of our dispersal. It is not messages you and I exchange that we desire. It is structures in which messages are exchanged that we want—a permanent hook-up, connection, contact. Looks, words, touches are forms of communication humans have devised to enter into such structures.

LVI

> Who is younger than I?

The contemptible twig?
that I was?

Yet nothing is precisely integrated, all is excessively overdetermined, not yet there, finally unrecognized. Beyond all rigidities of order, we are a site of disorder for seeing into an order that was built. We fit into it.

LVII

—but certainly
not for the university, what they publish
severally or as a group: clerks
got out of hand forgetting for the most part

It is the factory of production in the widest sense that determines the end result of any one thing produced within it. Parts circulate *en masse*, through the whole.

LVIII

He was 89 years old when he died, and doubtless had turned his farm over to his children, so that he retained only what he needed for his personal comfort: 24 shirts at .82½ cents, $19.88: 5 sheets, $7.00: 4 pillow cases, $2.12: 4 pair trousers, $2.00: 1 sheet, $1.37½: a handkerchief, $1.75…

The genius of industry was to cognize the system a new mode of production would create. Genius is the self-reflexive moment where information feeds back into knowledge in the fluid relation of part to whole.

There are no individuals but only so many as mass, absorbing the efforts of individual production. Fixity and motion are arrayed against the works and days of poets, those frustrated mountaineers whose end result is outside a totality they cannot comprehend.

## LVIX

but which he saw,
within himself—ice bound

and leaped, "the body, not until
the following spring, frozen in
an ice cake"

And what is poet? It is this incomprehensible linkage necessary to any totality. We must demand the right of the poet to represent her rightful place in an order that exceeds her, which she cannot comprehend. His speech was slurred to the point of incomprehension, there is not the hint of a ghost of order around him. The poet as incomprehensible register of the whole is linked to they who refuse any necessary order.

## LX

To make a start,
out of particulars
and make them general

Poet seeks other as definitively marked imprint of an order that exceeds them, by which it is disclosed.

# The Annotated "Plan B"

Damn the consequences!
Titanic loss drives market up—
Red states rule 1

Over blue states.
As a consequence of illogic
All can be winners!

In *Casino Royale.*
Do not mention Plan B
On social media.

Never underestimate
The power of data analytics
To fill in blanks.

[1] "Damn the torpedoes," from the Battle of Manila Bay, must be what American voters were thinking. My Facebook post when the event went south was "Titanic." Cf. *huge* or *yuge* as an index of loss; the sinking of the *Titanic*. The stock market gained after the event. The US is divided into Red states and Blue states, most notably after a map published in the *New York Times* during the contested election in 2000. American politics has been moving to one-party rule in Red states and Blue states for some time. See my poem on Bush II's reelection, "Blue States (After Fearing)."

[2] Winning versus losing as the metadiscourse of the event. Populism elects itself just as everyman can be a winner. Winning is not rational but circular, as being a *winner* is always a consequence of *winning*. In America, nothing succeeds like success. Decisionism is at the core of the event: meaning follows a result seen as decisive.

[3] Said person owned casinos in Atlantic City that went bankrupt; the James Bond film *Casino Royale* as a metaphor for American democracy; we are in the movies, a fantasy space. *Plan B* has many meanings, and will be repeated once every ten lines, as also will *Gleichschaltung*. One meaning: "to [ ] the president," which cannot be said on social media.

[4] Data analytics, of the sort pollsters use to assess the value of polling data, are applied retrospectively to gain prospective results. But a retrospective analysis is still prospectively unsure, as we have seen. Meaning in the event was a blank, waiting to be filled in by retrospective data analytics. The blanks are on forms that generate data, generating analytics that serve to confirm themselves.

The people according
To whom? Clock into their
Diurnal routine

And normalize.
*Gleichschaltung* freezes
The present moment

In a congealed frame.
Meaning merely the price
Of witnessing events.

To learn this word
Use it in conversation
Until it too is normal—

[5] The definition of the "people" is a retrospective determination based on data analytics. Pollsters attributed the final result to "demographics," the underlying data their analysis could not accurately represent. Once declared of "the people," a discourse is created on a temporal basis that works to normalize its constitution as such. The pressure to "normalize" is thus an attempt to constitute "the people" on the basis of the retrospective determination of data analytics. Everyday life will be the primary site for normalization, as I found out after the event in a series of interactions in doctor's offices, hair salons, auto repair shops, and hardware stores—as predictably as the sun courses in its diurnal round.

[6] Our political imperative of the present moment is to not "normalize," to resist by any means necessary the retrospective construction of a polity based on the result. *Gleichschaltung* is a term from the history of National Socialism, indicating the "switching over to the same" or "coordination" of both institutions, like Boy Scouts to Hitler Youth, and psychology, as when assimilated Jews would suddenly find themselves outed and excluded. We must resist any such attempt at coordination, as we saw with the Muslim travel ban. The word appears every ten lines, with shifting shades of meaning, to keep it in the mix of discourse but to undermine its application. *Gleichschaltung* is the name for a presentism we cannot allow.

[7] As a word *Gleichschaltung* works at the level of frame semantics, collapsing demographic data from multiple frames of reference into a single frame and a decisive result. Perhaps any witness to a complex and overdetermined event, such as a train wreck or the sinking of the *Titanic*, would condense meaning in this way. Therefore, meaning is decisive, as its event. Could the unpacking of meaning reverse the course of an event? The poem hopes it will.

[8] Meaning is use, after Wittgenstein, so if a word is used repeatedly it will take on the meaning of

Watching early returns
And reading *Armed Cell*
Until nothing is normal

All is weird and strange.
Combinatorial demographics—
Algorithmic decisions.

We break ourselves up
To produce more literature
For the illiterate.

Beyond category's reach
The abstraction of number
Lays waste

that use. *Gleichschaltung* could become normalized in this way, and spur normalization. But it could also become better known as a critical term for unpacking current politics. Hence, using the word *Gleichschaltung* could reverse its meaning as instrumental, as a critical tool.

[9] As I watched the returns, I picked up the latest issue of the post-Occupy little magazine *Armed Cell*. The semantic shift from *Armed Cell* to the event as it unfolded defamiliarizes normality but at the same time made it clear that all was lost. The magazine intends to pursue a post-crisis poetics, as a prospective affirmation, but we are not there yet.

[10] The decisive result of the event was a semantic shift that defamiliarized the ground of American politics and tried to reconstitute it in a fantasmatic form based on an abyss of meaning. Data algorithms traverse this abyss by reducing the polity to data, metadata, and profiles, which are mathematically combined through set operations to yield a result. But the result is finally "weird and strange."

[11] Poems—after the activism of Occupy—work at the micro-level of reversing fixed meanings and values, which they attempt to introduce into a population that has become ever more illiterate, reactive, and resistant to analytic thinking. Thus the turn of poetry to algorithmic micropolitics and the increased illiteracy of the populace may be dialectically linked. We ourselves are broken apart as singular agents, which is both the advantage and disadvantage of our analysis. What we produce is literature, but it breaks apart as literature due to the mass effect of popular illiteracy.

[12] There is a disconnect between the abstraction of data and the construction of categories for organizing it. Hence, data pulls away from the construction of categories, while any interpretation of a result depends on them. Data in and of itself becomes a form of wasteful excess, much like the death drive experienced in the pure winning and

Turns psychological.
*Gleichschaltung* repeats
Its deadly meaning.

Is that a thing
Or an image of one?
The image detaches

And spins as a segue
To Plan B as next segment
Of the narrative.

Aggregative informatics—
Yield qualitative results.
I use the word *advisedly*

losing at casinos. The event is nothing more than a deathward casino.

[13] There is a significant aspect of the death drive in the pure numbers of data analytics. As the event approached, one was addicted to polling data and metadata, checking for new results with increasing frequency. My anxiety became like that of an approaching fatal event, which the concept of *Gleichschaltung* depends on for its force. *Gleichschaltung* interprets the death drive in the making of a polity in which one part of the populace may be sacrificed or killed. So it happened in 1933-45, in which *Gleichschaltung* continued to repeat itself as ever deadlier, a terminating spiral.

[14] Data analytics is an attack on meaning in which language is dissociated from representation. Such a dissociation was also a part of said person's rhetoric, which reversed meanings within a single sentence. The indeterminacy of political rhetoric as representation is likewise mirrored in the abstraction of data analytics. A knowledge base brings together the thing represented and its form of representation, either word or image, while not being reducible to either. A knowledge base is a form of linking that conveys both the necessity and means of knowing. The politics of mere image—the simulacrum *même*—defeats knowledge as mere data.

[15] The repetition of images in the news cycle makes a simulacral sequence that substitutes for narrative but opens the possibility of an indeterminate event. The event's result, as a contingent but decisive image, may thus lead to Plan B in whatever form it presents itself—reversal of semantic field, mass revolt, impeachment. The means by which the event was decided might also be how it will be overturned.

[16] Quantity of information transforms into the quality of a result, and that is likewise true of an event in which every vote should count. But it is only the aggregate of votes that count—the individual vote not at all. The aggregate of information

Resulting in a shift
In the quality of life
As a cognitive process.

I use the word *terrified*
In a sentence that states
Nothing is normal.

License plate reads *BRUTEST*
A message in a bottle
Driving in Michigan

Windows rolled up.
And if he bicycles to work
He'd be called out 20

is a metadiscourse that is both unstable and decisive. Using a word on an individual basis—like casting a vote—is likewise contingent and undecidable; there is doubt and hesitation in the use of language at the level of the word, as it will never be equal to the sum total of information that results. One therefore cannot "speak" the truth of the event; it only happens in the way it does.

[17] The distancing of language on a word-to-word basis, however cautious we may be, in relation to the massive flux of data becomes a process of cognition in which the word as such is further dissociated, shifting the quality of life through its greater dissociation.

[18] The abyss of meaning that results becomes a precondition for terror—the dissociation of meaning in a decisive and violent event. But language may be a form of protest even in its dissociation, an index of the deathward tendency of information as undoing the norm that meaning established. Language is denormalization *même*.

[19] Thus all language at the level of word conveys an affect of brutality, like the Michigan license plate on an oversized SUV I saw while driving to the doctor's office. Michigan was a swing state that tilted the event as a result of signs—literally tens of thousands of signs supporters put out in Macomb County, terrifying the opposition but removed the next day. The condition of language in Michigan became as plain as a license plate on an oversized SUV.

[20] Meaning at the level of the word is an enclosed space, a car with windows rolled up. Alternate meanings cannot penetrate their windshield. A black poet in Berkeley, on the other hand, bicycled through the world without such protective isolation—only to result in being called out for "pedaling while black." Driving while black [DWB] is a frequent cause of arrest among African Americans, especially outside the neighborhoods in which they live. There had been a dramatic increase in racially and ethnically moti-

For pedaling while black.
    All data tends toward
        A common center

Of means-end rationality.
    *The Shining* screened in reverse
        Disappears into itself.

There is no comprehension;
    There is only computation.
        Autumn leaves

Blasted in virtual space.
    The flatline of the political
        Result of brute force

vated verbal and physical abuse during and after the event. I spotted the SUV in Franklin, Michigan, while the poet was called out for his race in Berkeley, California.

[21] Both SUV and bicycle are a part of the same cultural logic, irreducible to their metadata or to an aggregate analytics. As extremes together they point toward a mean of aggregate data that defines a commonality of the polis. Thus driving and bicycling are inherently political acts. The language I want captures that agency in the "making same" of all particularity.

[22] A cultural logic may be described through its means or extremes—the commodity form or race, class, and gender. The sum total of all instances of a cultural logic becomes a form of destructive rationality Theodor W. Adorno identified and warned us about. In a screening of Stanley Kubrick's *The Shining* at an artspace in Detroit, the artist projected the film from both ends simultaneously. At the midpoint of the film, the double projection coalesced into a single image—seeming to disappear as narrative continuity, forward or reverse. For one brief moment, the cultural logic of *The Shining* declared itself as its own fixed image, a metadiscourse that effaced its own narrative. In like fashion, double or contradictory cultural logics dissolve into static, atemporal images and then reemerge.

[23] Such static, atemporal images that dissolve and destroy narratives and contexts make interpretation and comprehension intractable. We can only add up the results, forcing quality of meaning in the direction of quantity of data. Thus autumn leaves falling in profusion can only helplessly show themselves as they fall. No single leaf can communicate its narrative; loss of aggregate meaning is inevitable.

[24] Simulacral falling leaves, both real and imagined, define and fill a space of potential that may only be understood as a terrifying event. What if all the leaves in the world were to fall right now? That would be a disaster greater than the sinking

A kind of numbness
Men made of cardboard
Paralyzed inertness.

Plan B: birth control
Countermeasure to terminate
Unwanted presidency.

The darkest hour
May be just before dawn.
I refuse to normalize

High-low distinction
That makes class politics
A joke for the ages.

of the *Titanic*. Yet we normalize the falling of leaves on a seasonally adjusted basis. Politics too is the normalization of terror and loss, destroying narrative and cognition on the flatline of the incommunicable.

[25] The communicative aporia we are within results in a massive onslaught of data that resists any determination but terror and loss as a kind of paralysis or inertness. We become the "men made of cardboard" Ezra Pound wrote about, the victims of modernity who become its constitutive parts.

[26] Another meaning for Plan B is the morning after pill to terminate a potential pregnancy. During the Vietnam War, a protest sign seen at rallies begged the president to "pull out Dick, like your mother should have." Rolling back reproductive rights is a major item on said person's agenda. Pink pussy hats were everywhere at protest rallies around the world the morning after the event. Such countermeasures, too, could terminate an unwanted presidency.

[27] There is hope, even in the worst of circumstances. Things often seem at their bleakest just before they improve. An adage or maxim or expression that is hopeful: *this too shall pass*. An irretrievable memory from a sequence of song lyrics lost in the cultural database. Initially used as a homiletic in the seventeenth century. My refusal to normalize is an expression of hope, even as I slip into utter darkness.

[28] By magic the interests of the rulers are those of the working class? The coal miners voting for Thatcher; union democrats for Reagan? What I refuse to normalize is the betrayal of class interest as a class politics, as reportedly in the working class's tilt right in the event. The use of class to cover for authoritarianism and racism is a specious contradiction. The revolution brings the dawn from the darkness of class politics as the ages stand witness.

They refuse to vote
        Their interest because
                They do not know it.

*Gleichschaltung* follows
        Shame and humiliation
                With brute force.

In the reception room
        All the patients are men
                Wearing their class

On their sleeves.
        The data are an event
                But not our destiny.

[29] The origin of cultural studies is from the need to explain this crucial ideological turnaround. In Michigan the center of ideological denial is in Macomb County, the white working class that voted Wallace in 1968 and Reagan in 1980. Politics is currently based more on the "refusal to know" than any avowal of interest.

[30] *Gleichschaltung* exploits an ideological weakness that is lived in affective terms. It begins by exploiting a defensive reaction to ego-threatening force, demonstrating a bad compromise formation. It follows the psychic threat of force, and the dissociation that results, with a real instance of force. The first concentration camps appeared in March 1933; cf. the recent discussion of using the National Guard to round up and deport undocumented immigrants.

[31] The ego-threatening force of shame and humiliation undoes a masculinity that wants to be hard and invulnerable, as it believes it should be. Working class men in a doctor's office, in denial of their need, show their vulnerability for all to see as receptionists hover nearby. The rise of the "white male" is only a symptom.

[32] The evidence of the senses is dissociated from the compilation of data. Working class men in a doctor's office are not supposed to be in need of medical care as a social good, even as they depend on it and benefit from it. The predictions of data analytics may be the ideological occasion for a political putsch, but they do not eliminate social need at the core.

50/50 Rule of means/end
Neither one achieved
No matter how many

Voted—the numbers
Refuse to add up
To a predicted measure.

We feel the data
As an inertial weight
Making things strange

Out of all proportion.
They cry out for Plan B
To rescue themselves.

[33] A 50/50 Rule for poetics and pedagogy is to combine one part of what is previously known and one part of what is yet to be understood. A form of means/end rationality as the result of a dialectic of known and unknown. In the 50/50 Rule of American politics, all interests split on demographic lines as evenly as possible, so that the most narrow interest tilts the vote to the desired result. This too is a form of social rationality, but in a destructive not progressive form. In the event, neither side achieved 50%, with the result that the lack of any majority gave us a minority government.

[34] The lack of consensus becomes the guarantee of consensus, as an outcome of the event. Insofar as the popular vote did not add up to a decisive victory, it opened the way for the imposition of a decision. In the lack of a quantitative mandate, the qualitative Mandate of Heaven imposes itself with redoubled force. The positivizing of the negative by force is the origin of an authoritarian mandate in which the electoral college outweighed the preponderance of numbers, as an ideological necessity.

[35] The contradictory claims of an event that was both won and lost renders the populace continually vulnerable to interpretive claims based on the manipulation of data analytics. The sheer volume and mass of data counters any rational justification, leading to dissociation that is the first step in a political putsch. Any argument is as compelling as any other, and anything can be justified on that basis.

[36] The lack of justification creates a wildness in public discourse that opens the way to countermeasures that, by the same illogic, overturn the result in a desperate act of rescue. Oppositely, the lack of any justification could make all countermeasures appear as another Plan B—desperate and lacking any possibility. The cries for rescue were plaintive and audible as the *Titanic* went down, but to no avail.

My South Asian daughter
Cannot weep out of state
And drives nonstop.

Open fields of meaning
Hemmed in by borders
Increasingly insecure.

After Article 50
They invoke *Gleichschaltung*
As an irreversible force

Of inevitable decline—
Compelled they cannot help
Their own destruction.

[37] This terrible event has hurt those dear to me. There were many tears on the morning after. My South Asian daughter-in-law in Chicago feared for her safety, as did many in her community house. She thought of getting in a car and driving nonstop across Indiana as a way to be safe. Another could not communicate their distress and withdrew from contact for days until it ended. On the flip side of the nonstop input of dissociated data and bad results, ghosts of injury work through shame and humiliation. Solidarity with people of color who were hurt in this way follows the decision structure of the poem.

[38] The horizon of an open field was a moment of poetic and political ideology that worked at the time. But meaning is now bounded in any understanding of it, even by the insecurity of its boundaries. The insecurity of boundaries puts pressure on meaning, becoming a prior condition in need of an address. The best location to address the insecure boundaries of meaning is at the border between things—not in any open field of expansive logic.

[39] Insecurity about the boundaries of meaning, as cultural and political logic, led to the UK vote to the leave the EU, although a decisive act of exit (Article 50) was not yet invoked. The symbolic violence of Article 50 to deny difference in a global world also leads to the symbolic violence of *Gleichschaltung* to enforce the same, coordinating abjection of other to likeness. Where boundaries are confused, the act of expulsion is a self-wounding denial of self that wishes for the certainty of a lost boundary.

[40] *Gleichschaltung* is a destructive force, even as it implies a return to the same. For Freud the aim of all life as death is a homeostasis of the organism. Homeostasis of the political body is its death drive, its constitutive undoing. The fantasy of sameness as a politics is only achieved through one form of destruction or another. Like lemmings, we are compelled to seek it, year after year.

Domination follows competition
Force guile irony stress—
Even if it is what is

Do not normalize
Seek Plan B if only to
Recalculate your life.

Expatriation follows alienation
To find an alternative
Existence elsewhere.

Nothing follows nothing:
The Rights of Woman traduced
By Lords of Misrule.

[41] Under capitalism, homeostasis is made possible in economic terms, where all is competition. But in political terms, it is achieved through force and domination. Political economy in neoliberalism is an admixture of the market with force, seen as all manner of compulsion. The bottom line is an unstable result in both senses, a result that must be contested. The circulation of capital leads to homeostasis in political terms.

[42] The contradiction between politics as force and the market as competition requires us to recalculate our interest in both senses. Plan B is the moment of recalculation and adjustment within a process that is unceasingly advancing toward the end of destruction as its form of renewal. The measured progress of one's life is the only contrary to the cultural logic of destruction.

[43] Such measured progress is only possible from a position outside the cultural logic we are within. The alienation needed to enact Plan B may lead to expatriation to Canada, Europe, or parts unknown. For the surrealists, *l'existence est ailleurs*—the eternal return of the same is an inscription of unreason as *aliené*, a becoming other of reason in madness. Alienation leads to expatriation as a form of existence elsewhere.

[44] The sign of madness is *nothing* as a consequence of itself—there is no motivation but one that consumes everything as a version of the same. For women, refusal to adhere to the reproduction of the same leads to exclusion from the Symbolic as *nothing*. Women may either fit into the Symbolic or become nothing in the fantasy of the libertine, the Lord of Misrule. The libertine's attack on the body is his denial of the woman who gave him birth, whose nurture he needs, a demand to recover a lost object he will never regain. To deny the rights of woman is

The Rights of Man—
A gutted document
Of burned parchment

*Dokumentationzentrum*
A new destination for tourism
And skatepunk culture.

I never signed
Any nondisclosure agreement
Only to act as if we had

The movie rights
To *Gleichschaltung* distributed
As a general good—

a self-betrayal; the libertine's self-denial is his destruction.

[45] The denial of gender at the heart of a politics of domination leads to the evisceration of the concept of Man. There is self-betrayal in any assertion of a Right, becoming destruction in the immolation of history that produced Man. Woman as procreation and history as production disappear into the same convulsive act. The Rights of Man and Woman can only emerge in the convulsive act of revolution, the culmination of Plan B. With Plan B, the Rights of Man and Woman will phoenix-like arise from the ashes of conflagration.

[46] Decades after the first wave of *Gleichschaltung* had run its course, the politics of *Vergangenheitsbewältigung* (coming to terms with the past) advanced all over Germany. Reeducation campaigns target teenage skatepunks on the disused concrete of the Nürnberg rallies. Skatepunks and Holocaust tourists fund an economy of loss that produces new meanings. The media display in the *Dokuzentrum* defines and uses *Gleichschaltung* in a sentence, along with narratives and images that interpret its force. This poem is an advance payment on a *Dokuzentrum* as witness to our destructive moment of *Gleichschaltung*.

[47] The libertine's wives were forced to sign a nondisclosure agreement as the final end to their nuptial accord. In this case the rights of women were abridged by contract not to disclose the truth of their arrangements. If only the rights of man could refuse any such contractual abridgement of the right to speak to this brutal domination and mendacity! I want to speak truth to power, as my right to do so may be. But media obtains the rights to my story even before I know to exercise them. As a libertine Rupert Murdoch believes he has a contract on human interest that absorbs even my story, which he controls offshore in the Bahamas.

[48] All of our *Stürm und Drang* is scripted for the movies; our suffering is to recover the rights to the primary motivations that move us. The end-

A classroom lecture
In the very courthouse
Where trials took place

Overturning their result.
I refuse to normalize—
And this is my Right. 50

Wake up to a new order
And Plan B as alternative
Ghost assembly line.

"Where the dead walked
And the living were made
of metadata"—

less loop of denial is an enactment of the eternal return as movie contract to distribute our story to all markets domestic or foreign. *Gleichschaltung* is the boilerplate contract that permits the exploitation of our suffering for the greater good of the movie-going masses. The movie industry imitates a form of *Gleichschaltung* as it overwrites our suffering with the story of ourselves it represents.

[49] We need a form of advance reeducation that will inure us to our suffering before it occurs. On visiting the *Gerichtssaal* of the *Nürnberger Prozesse*, we take part in the dismantling of *Gleichschaltung* through the renewal of a legal standard—in the obligation to reject an order that does not adhere to universal standards, thus trumping any call to the nation state as our obligation.

[50] In the Vietnam War, I adhered to an obligation to refuse participation in an unjust, illegal, and racist war of extermination. My obligation trumped national duty, at the peril of arrest and incarceration. In the end, it turns out I was right; my refusal turned out to be my right. The refusal of normalization in *Gleichschaltung* is a prospective right of historical obligation. We have an ethical obligation not to normalize.

[51] The new order of displaced politics demands an alternative counter-mode of production. The ghost of Marx that Jacques Derrida wrote about, where "the time is out of joint," becomes a sequential realization, a new assembly line for an alternative polity. The ghost of Marx persists in the sequential unfolding of its logic. The new order is contested by a shadow economy that unfolds as it undermines it. In the new order, *1984* and *Brave New World* will be reprinted in large popular editions.

[52] At the ending of Ezra Pound's *Cantos*, a final moment of self-exculpation is preceded by a phrase that aligns the US with the *NS* state: "in meiner Heimat." *Heimat* was a television miniseries in Germany in 1984 that helped open the way for "coming to terms with the past." The poet is in

Fact *were it* otherwise
In the subjunctive case
Of mood alteration.

In a windowless building—
You know the one!—
They conduct surveillance

On foreign elements
Floating to the surface
Of dark, polluted streams. 55

New voting machine installed
As they foil sabotage
At the name-brand hotel

denial of his past, and ascribes his errors only to others. All political actors outside one's personal tragedy are merely made of cardboard, the missing agents the failure of the poem purports to contest. Such reversals add up to the data of politics and poetry, allowing us to draw inferences, evaluate, and act. Failure thus becomes possibility as fact.

[53] A fact is a modal—a condition of possibility. All facts are interpretive, for Nietzsche, and there is no fact without multiple, competing perspectives. The realization of the fundamental lack of ground of what we thought were facts is a subjunctive modality with affective consequences. Our change in mood is the result of an ungrounding of facts as conditions of possibility.

[54] We can imagine the center of surveillance to be a large, grey, windowless concrete building—anyone will recognize this building even without having seen it. The headquarters of the CIA in Langley, Virginia, is not a windowless building; the Lubyanka in Moscow, now home to the FSB, is lavishly painted and redecorated, with windows on every floor. The real windowless building must be "elsewhere." Poetry itself has been described as a "windowless monad," but here it is all windows.

[55] A dark polluted stream carries the effluents of our mode of production downriver, including the human detritus it swept up to become its labor force. The abjection of their labor is a consequence of their darkening and vice versa. Masters of industry see them only as pollution once their labor is done and used up. Marx saw the *petite bourgeoisie* as scum floating on the river of capitalism—and these scum caused the flotation of many dark bodies.

[56] Democracy is a contradiction in a security state, where there can be no open discussion; security measures attach to the voting machine. But it is is the enabling condition of a market society, where naming rights to stadiums and hotels seduce the population that pays to enter. "Pay to play" is the principle by which one needs to pro-

With no ties to Putin
Or the Russian state—
Our results are clean!

As clean as *Gleichschaltung*!
Cleansing the nation
Of foreign elements

Unwanted, unneeded, undesired
Undocumented, unrequited
Unrepresented people

Numbering in the millions
Are affected by decree
And rumor of affect

vide monetary compensation to come close to power. Domestic lobbyists and foreign entrepreneurs book the name-brand hotel for years in advance to gain influence.

[57] Influence proceeds by denial of influence, by destabilizing public discourse in absentia. Lies are a means of self-cleansing in the bath of the other. An unverifiable cause is the guarantee of the clean results of a campaign of distortion. In "The Purloined Letter" the truth is visible on the surface; the letter is on the table. Of course there was no influence on the event by Putin or the Russian State: *Quod erat demonstrandum.* At the end of every mathematical proof: the proof that lies are truth.

[58] "Switching over" in *Gleichschaltung* is motivated by the desire to cleanse via exclusion. The *NS* jurist Carl Schmitt theorized the right of a state to define itself by externalizing and eliminating threats. In Gulf War II, Bush's legal apologists adopted Schmitt's "state of exception" as its rationale for treating captured persons housed at Guantanamo Bay as "unlawful combatants"—outside the jurisdictional oversight of law, national or international. A nation is defined, as a result, by a politics of exclusion; there is no other order.

[59] The prefix *un-* signifies *not* or *opposite of, contrary to.* It is used in words that have a meaning that negates that of the base word. Those who are excluded may thus be defined negatively by the mere imposition of a prefix; they may believe the word applies to them. They may lack proper documentation or no longer be needed for political or economic purposes. They may as a result not have any political representation, and be subjected to removal by legal means backed up by force.

[60] The change of a legal or political designation by mere prefix can affect millions of people. Language constructs discourse at a minimal level of signification in such a case. Language is the law of large numbers, of all that it defines. One decree can reach millions through the force and extent of language. The affects that result are distributed

In organized state of denial
As new affect akin to
Boredom and hate.

It is boring in Macomb County—
We need some excitement
To flip our pick-up trucks

And the entire state
Of its unexcited majorities
Whose quietude is fear.

massively through the medium that decrees them univocally.

[61] Negation is promulgated through language not only by decree—by the transvaluation of positivity to its opposite—but through a systematic denial of consequences. In this case, the consequences are naturalized in language, always already there as a matter of definition. Language, like the bourgeoisie, is the most revolutionary element—but also the most conservative. The affects that result from the distribution of denial through language become existential—as with Heidegger's account of boredom as primordial affect of enduring existence before language—but also passional, a feeling state that needs to abject others. We need more research on the relation of boredom as asignifying versus hate as an act of speech.

[62] The best place to gauge Heidegger's account of boredom as a politics would be Macomb County, Michigan—home to Ford F-150 pick-up trucks, NRA members, and white supremacists. The *anomie* of the "white working class" leads to rejection of class and union politics, resulting in votes on racial and cultural lines. Knowing that Macomb County voted for white supremacist George Wallace in 1968, for union-buster Ronald Reagan in 1980, and helped defeat its opponent in the primary, Republican operatives encouraged massive and intimidating display of partisan support. The result was overwhelming, 54 to 42%, generating enough votes to flip the usually Blue state Red. The result also depended on a depressed voter turnout in urban areas such as Detroit.

[63] Only Macomb County saw such a coordinated effort to excite the white working class as base and depress other voting blocs. The rest of the state followed the 50/50 rule of clinging to the faultline between Blue urban counties and Red rural ones. The lack of excitement for the event in the state overall helped deliver the result through one county. The population overall seemed to doubt the event would reflect their interests, and feared the political discourse of othering it unleashed.

Seize Bucks County
By the throat and deliver
The results on deadline

Like a dog returning
To its vomit in a Bible Study
Group of deplorables.

"Naaaaw, I don't see anything
Racist in this result
But I got a new Idee—

[64] Philadelphia suburb Bucks County was also a target for Republicans. While the four largest counties went Blue by substantial majorities, the margin in Bucks County was less than 1%, allowing rural counties going Red to deliver the state. The slippery slope of low turnout where not expected was decisive—but the opposite of any coordinated plan. Pennsylvania slipped due to lack of enthusiasm for Democrats, who were unable to take fate by the throat—in a state they had regarded as their firewall.

[65] Televangelists like Jimmie Swaggart are fond of the phrase "as a dog returning to its vomit, so a fool repeats his folly" (Proverbs 26:11). As a repulsive image, the proverb inculcates the shame that returns a sinner to the path. Swaggart himself confessed to extramarital affairs in an effusion of self-castigation that was unpleasant to witness but that he hoped would inspire conversions to his church. Taking the trope from the religious Right, the event was staged as a pool of vomit that voters needed to reject as a matter of faith. As a "basket of deplorables," such voters might affirm their status as sinners and thus seek their own conversion rather than be labeled as such by pious Democrats—a major mistake in understanding populist psychology as fueled by *ressentiment* and victimhood. The Bible study group becomes the prototype for a community of interpretation based on debasement and need for spiritual renewal.

[66] For Ezra Pound, after William James, "genius is the capacity to see ten things when the ordinary man sees one"; for Aristotle, "there is no great genius without a touch of madness." Pound's Uncle Remus dialect masked denial of race in its ventriloquism of the masses. Mainstream media denied racism as primary cause of the election result, while the evident racism it mobilized was irreducible for many. The category of "class" suddenly appeared in mainstream discourse as a result. In the film *Irma Vep*, Jean-Pierre Léaud as the Director denies that any "idée" can be responsible for genius, yelling, "What do I want with an Idee" before collapsing from nervous exhaustion.

Let's call it *class*"—Plan B
To deny over breakfast
Normalized to explain

How we tipped the plates
Pancakes all over the table
To achieve this result!

Perfidy of mediated state
Returning to normalize
Discourse under control.

The New *Gleichschaltung*
Being barely perceptible
Everything is normal

[67] While mainstream media eschews Marxism, *class* as an explanation is everywhere without being fully explained, consistently used, or part of a larger analysis. Class politics as Plan B from a mainstream perspective would be incoherent, a site for denial of larger politics that is normalized as a nonexplanation—thus rendering moot any Marxist "impulse to action." Terms like *class* may be used to legitimate the status quo in the absence of any alternative—such as we desire with Plan B!

[68] The expression *tippy plate* means one whose reason is unsound; cf. *cracked pot*. The good life in America may be visualized as a product package depicting a happy family sharing a steaming pile of pancakes Mother just made. Alt-Right editor Steve Bannon's dark vision of political renewal demands overturning the status quo in order to radicalize the population. For those of his ilk, populism can only be achieved by trauma, a train wreck of the good life for the middle class. The disruption of a politics of unreason intends an uncertain, unstable political goal.

[69] The battle cry of the New Right over the past two decades has been for "fair and balanced" media coverage—so that untenable political claims and distorted views become equivalent to rational discussion. Alexis de Tocqueville's "tyranny of the majority" describes a situation in which the majority is understood as quantity not quality, and the truth of discourse is a mere average. The 50/50 Rule in its generalization of false equality—equality of condition, not of right—thus tends toward incompetence and corruption as the normalized state. Political control depends on normalization above all.

[70] The switching-over of *Gleichschaltung* is now continuous and uninterrupted, an algorithm combining data mining, niche marketing, and discourse construction in its seamless micromanagement. Normalization and perception have become strictly opposed; raising language and cognition to perception is a fundamental politics. Democracy is tending toward a collective state of mind that

The New Detroit unfolds
Permanently on hold
With nothing to build.

Nothing, *nichevo, nichts, rien*
In thirty-seven languages
None mutually intelligible—

Vietnamese, Croatian, Arabic, Hmong
Observed at a voting booth
Next to exit signs.

Plan B is to take a vacation
Start writing autobiography
Limit oneself to memoirs

continually adapts to an increased level of threat that is excluded from the body politic, tending toward destruction. Democracy in such a scenario is trending toward fascism.

[71] Detroit's renewal comes after decades of stagnation and depopulation. The New Detroit is an equilibrium state between new buildings and commercial interests and the continuing decline of neighborhoods, often 90% abandoned buildings and void spaces. Narratives of progress in Detroit compete with this persistence of decline, ending in a topography where time has evaporated. *Nothing* in Detroit is a permanent, ateleological fact, even as we watch new arenas and casinos spring up.

[72] Heidegger's "What Is Metaphysics" sees the anxiety of the *nothing* as a source for a metaphysics of Being. Each language has a special word for this *nothing*, unintelligible to each other as they are founded in nonexistence. Speakers of at least thirty-seven languages participating in the event often found no one on the ballot who represented their interests. In the Tower of Babel, language is a particularism by which one cannot accede to the universal. The Esperanto movement sought to correct heteroglossia by creating a universal language out of a hybrid of Indo-European languages. Heidegger asked, "How goes it with the Nothing," which must be answered in a specific language such as English, Russian, German, or French—in the nonexistence of a concept. Between languages meaninglessness is a precondition of meaning and its ultimate horizon.

[73] In some states, ballots are printed in multiple languages, determined by local demography, while some states have English-only ballots. A candidate for president was admonished to "speak English," though the Constitution does not require one must. In my precinct, voters were directed to the exit after their votes were recorded by signs in multiple languages, but the ballot itself was in English.

[74] One response to the normalization of the

Only to be hacked online
Their emails purloined
And publicly humiliated.

It's a Mongolian Sausage!
Return of the repressed
Of my poetic lineage.

"Put shit in a stocking
Swing it around your head
Until everyone goes home."

event is to ignore it entirely, consider only one's own interests, maximize one's benefits, and pursue lifetime goals regardless. In the end, one has the option to write autobiography but only through an act of political denial. Thus I concluded my poem "Mode Z," anticipating the present moment in 1980, with the pointedly ironic line "start writing autobiography," but that negation is never the whole story.

[75] Our private data is ultimately discoverable, searchable, and capable of being purloined. The data functions as a source of shame and humiliation for anyone whom has it exposed. The publication of thousands of the opponent's emails was meant to shame and humiliate her. While no information was gained, and no charges were filed, the damage it caused was permanent. Autobiography as narrative is not the final horizon of the event; data as nonnarrative was the effective cause leading to the result.

[76] The New York poet Ted Berrigan liked to flirt with gestures of omnipotence such as the poetic trope of a shit-filled stocking. Said person opined that he could stand in the middle of Fifth Avenue and shoot someone and still win in the event. Poetry and politics meet at the intersection of fantasies of invulnerability. Poetry and politics diverge at the dissociation or enactment of such fantasies. The lineage of avant-garde poetry is a political unconscious whose repression is released by dark tropes. Poets internalize the order of poets, just as the people internalize the order of presidents.

[77] Ted Berrigan's definition of a Mongolian Sausage is the metadata of a transgressive act in its impossibility and inutility—by definition, it is an act that can never be performed. Making a gigantic stink in a public situation is one way to define and control it. That "everyone will agree" as the hallmark of the aesthetic is certain when the object of the agreement is disgust. Transgression and disgust, moral turpitude and outrage, replace the ambiguity of communities of taste where *no*

*Gleichschaltung* like that—
When it rains it pours
Shit or Shinola as *shit*.

These are just words
And those were just words
And words have an effect.

No damage no results
Means no pain no gain
Means no lumps no vote.

*one can decide*. Aesthetic community as a politics is founded on a negative distribution of the senses. That *everyone will go home* is our current politics, opening the warehouse to corporate greed.

[78] *Gleichschaltung* is the cover-up and denial of a situation that stinks to the high heavens—the violence of normalization making everyone go home and lock their doors. "When it rains it pours": a young girl under an umbrella on a salt box. The situation outside is perpetual outrage to the senses that continues and increases in intensity. As a result the people cannot tell *shit* from *shinola*; their senses have been turned around. The violence of normalization is founded on the senses' revolt, stomachs regurgitating and bowels evacuating until no one can watch. This is the poetry that founds our politics, just as *Shinola* is the name brand for New Detroit.

[79] How much damage can be done with words? A great deal: cesspools of racism, misogyny, and xenophobia can be unleashed with mere words. Our confidence in the future could be augmented or destroyed by mere words. War could be declared by the use of certain words—a nuclear catastrophe that would destroy us all. The concept of *nuclear winter* is itself a fact of language—it has never been realized or seen. The fact of possibility and its undoing is the power of words. Words can change everything for the worst; or they can be summoned to change all for the best.

[80] Language is a risk that can never be a mere metadiscourse of neutrality. Language takes something and gives it back, on a visceral and embodied level. Without the violence of language, no comprehension may result. The distribution of the senses happens only when they are redistributed, which requires the use of force. Transferred to politics: the results we want will never follow a neutral procedure, just as the results they got were predicated on the threat of unreason, mendacity, and injury.

Triumph of triumphalism—
Futurity of crystal gazing
As medium of nonbeing.

A tip of the old iceberg
Of coordinated fantasy
Where the unstable go off

In hysterical bursts
Catastrophic incoherence
Roiling underneath.

[81] Either poetic or political triumphalism raises itself up *by its own petard*. It is *the proof of its own pudding*; the result of its own making is the achievement of a result. The result is not merely an empty foreshadowing of futurity but a violent eruption into the present, making nonbeing out of what was there before. Poetic or political triumph is transformative and transgressive, establishing a brutal continuity of language that others our being. Politics as poetry is the violent triumph of present over futurity as a medium for normalization. Poetry as politics changes course for futurity.

[82] Underneath all language and expression is a vast reservoir of conflicted and unexpressed feeling states that may erupt and destroy us at any time. Poets and politicians access and deploy this reservoir, on which the teachings of professors and psychoanalysts depend. Fantasy is a looming mass of submerged feeling states that, when accessed and deployed in a coordinated way, create a force of enormous capacity. The radical, unstable repression of that which lurks beneath ends in an explosive eruption, *a train wreck waiting to happen*. We see little versions of such an explosive train wreck as going off around us for some time. The Lac-Mégantic rail disaster in Quebec occurred at 01:15 EDT on 6 July 2013; millions of gallons of crude oil burned in the town for weeks.

[83] The triumphal emergence of poetry or politics is hysterical—it is the truth of the release of repression. Underneath the individual outburst lie decades of unaddressed desires and needs seeking acknowledgment and release—our "unfulfilled democratic demands." Underneath the earth's surface lie pools of magma that come periodically to the surface. The energy of repression is based on its lack of organization, inaccessibility to expression. Liquifying all that is solid and known, the energy of repression is at its most destructive.

Do I want to look at the news?
Do I need to? “Stalwarts
Try to Focus on Policy.”

In *Edmund Fitzgerald* weather
With 18-foot breakers
Breaking them in half

Result of a shallow floor.
Everything is adverbial—
That’s how it’s done.

[84] John Lennon’s “I read the news today” is a truth for the ages, a moment glimpsed outside of all time. The news once meant that which was timely and relevant; now it is what is continuous, inevitable, resistant to change. The *news* is no longer the *New*, becoming the grim reaper of habitual (mis)understanding. Utilities such as water, heat, electricity, and waste removal now include the provision of data services and news. To walk away from the infrastructural grid was a countercultural fantasy that is now strictly impossible. Headlines communicate lack of comprehension rather than any clarification of fact. The fact of incomprehension is our daily news, the social provision of our symbolic infrastructure.

[85] After Che Guevara and Slavoj Žižek, we might say “One, two, many disasters!” Just as the *Titanic* stands as synecdoche for the modern, the *Edmund Fitzgerald* symbolizes the state. Just as Walt Whitman imagined *years of the modern*, we might visualize enormous wave formations breaking our conveyances in half. The *Edmund Fitzgerald* departed with a cargo of taconite ore from Superior, Wisconsin, 9 November 1975. She might have fallen victim to high waves of the storm, suffered structural failure, been swamped with water entering her hatches, experienced topside damage, broken in two, or shoaled in a shallow part of Lake Superior.

[86] “All bottoms are false,” the poet Bill Berkson wrote, criticizing the desire for foundations. There is no bottom, but what is below may surge up nonetheless. The shallow floor of Lake Superior broke the *Edmund Fitzgerald* in half if the trough of the wave reached low. All is motion; no object is secure but is subject to its law and fate. *Motion* as a unifying concept has nonidentity and contradiction at its core. In capitalism it is the *motion* of capital that results in its destructive force. The *Edmund Fitzgerald* is a synecdoche for the destructive processes of capitalism that made Detroit the evacuation of meaning found in its physical state. Manipulating the *motion* of destructive force becomes the art of poetry and politics.

There is no floor or ground—
Level playing field
Opens to an abyss

Fair and balanced news—
With any nonsense analysis
As good as any other.

*Gleichschaltung* is this:
I compel content to yield
And cut out their tongues.

[87] *Years of the modern* substitutes an *abyss* for what was *ground*; critical theory brings them together as necessary attributes of the same. Between *abyss* and *ground*, in their confusion or exchange, lies an open field of fictive possibility we may identify with the poetic act. Such fiction of the possibility of equivalence between incommensurate states becomes a site for their normalization. A threat of the *abyss* conjoins certainty of *ground* as cover-up of force and denial in a return to the same.

[88] The 50/50 Rule extended to *news* means that the patently false and the demonstrably true coexist in the unity of opposites. The Hegelian underpinnings of an antidemocratic state are the irony of mere juxtaposition as a condition of truth—the truth represented by the state. *Nonsense* has its structural logic in ungrounding claims for the higher order of the state. All claims to truth result in the reinforcement of a higher order by the mere fact they cannot be proved. The demand for *fair and balanced news*, insisted on since the Millennium, was the vehicle for the New Right's takeover of the state.

[89] For Charles Olson, *polis* follows the deictic pronoun *this*, that when deployed, compels the town to yield in asymmetrical conformity. Poetic sovereignty is the content and force of the deictic pronoun. Muthologos is oral form, the vehicle of the force that compels *polis*. The threat of the sovereign's force is to cut out their tongues—a denial of speech as submission to the state. Orality negates content in a display of force that makes the poet a synecdoche for ruler. The demos survives as countermovement to deixis, keeps its mouth shut, continues writing. *Gleichschaltung* is a poetics of self-evidence underpinned by the threat of force. The content of all projection is forced on us, while its motive force in violence is denied.

The flip side of Plan B
Complete normalization
As if nothing happened

The national anthem
At sporting events—
Be seated at your peril.

Beyond the family romance
Of dysfunction, I'm sorry—
No extra caring here.

[90] Plan B is the reversal of the process of *Gleichschaltung*. Normalization erases the threat of violence as it generalizes it throughout the *polis*. Plan B restores the underlying turbulence that led to the desire for its eradication. The population cannot tolerate turbulence; the *polis* is turbulence *même*. Lately roiling with waves, the calm surface of the lake betrays its storms. This storm cannot be normalized: bring it on.

[91] Just as the violent asymmetry of the national anthem compels normalization, the high note always stands out as a mark of distinction and sovereignty that transcends its false occasion. Soul singers interpret the high note as transcendence; rockers render it thickly material. When conditions are right, it is our right not to stand for the national anthem as a mark of distinction and sovereignty that is lacking in its interpretation. Violence of the crowd surges up on all sides of the seeming betrayal of collectivity that its own values have authorized.

[92] The *family romance* is projective identification: we see cast on the big screen of *what is* a *not-I* that shapes my formative condition. All the elements are in place; the movie runs as manifold versions of the self play out who we are. Who we are is the dysfunction of our need for projection, for putting something *out there* that needs to be recognized *in here*. No apologies will be given for the need for projective identification, which outstrips any capacity for empathy in the *greed that they are alive*. Greedy clinging projections run our national life, and we believe that they are us. Where once *polis* ran on fumes of *bellum omnium contra omnes, the war of all against all* projects our singular destinies onto an unfolding screen of denying, uncaring abstraction.

Does poetry make a bubble
Of like-mined *simpaticos*
Foreign elements excluded?

Do we speak to the converted
Or the statistically lapsed
When they get over it?

Now use the word *reprobate*:
An unprincipled person—
Rogue, rascal, scoundrel 95

[93] Poetry confronts *polis* with a contrary commonwealth of *who we are*, a community of *like* in the exclusion of *unlike*. People like us, as in the song by Talking Heads, are the basis of liberal polity: so we ask, *who are we?* In digital environments, truth bubbles form that filter the news and protect communities from messages they do not want to receive. Only those with sympathetic views will be admitted to the algorithm—thus rendering foreign and strange all those excluded by it. The proper response to the truth bubble is to redirect the algorithm to smash the state—a thumbnail definition of the theory of Plan B. It is not to be found in the defensive posture of community formed as principle of denial.

[94] Truth bubbles filter out negative content and speak only to those in alignment or conformity, preparing the way for *Gleichschaltung* as cognitive processing. The authoritarian and communitarian fuse in the psychic fantasies of the populace. Demographics strain their algorithms at the 50/50 border between one state and another, working tirelessly to fold errant meanings into one category or another. Those outside the algorithm have a perilous identity, *neither fish nor fowl*, a hybridity that is either recognized as a new data point or cast into the rubbish heap of history. Algorithms leave no choice but to seek *like* after *like*, until the very function of the model is called into question. In the end, "the model" organizing the data failed to predict the outcome of the event, opening the way for decisions and outcomes not shaped by it.

[95] There is a *bad actor* at the heart of every algorithm, and the machinic parsing of *like* and *unlike* gives him free reign. There was a time in the past when people behaved like this: in the *ancien régime* as domain of The Libertine. There the fuckers of destiny held sway, deploying *lettres de caché* to impose their errant will on those of lesser class: milkmaids, shepherds, servant girls, livery men consumed in abandon. Language has a word for such moral cretins: the *reprobate* as the sum total of the attributes it assumes. Bad actors are *fuckers*, counting the bodies of victims. A dictionary gives us the means at their disposal—all the ways we have become undone by them. Under algorithmic searches lie the bad actors of the *ancien régime*, searching their victims in the order of words; metadata guides them on their way toward

Miscreant, good-for-nothing, villain
Wretch, rake, degenerate
Libertine, debauchee.

And raise the *Edmund Fitzgerald*!
A good ship and true—
From a mill in Wisconsin

Fully loaded for Cleveland.
Waves broke over the railing
Gales of November slashing.

new and unusual conquests. The demographics of metadata is a Sadean scene of seduction, betrayal, capture, use.

[96] Piling up synonyms for *bad actor* creates an antonymic countermovement insofar as his misdeeds cannot be believed. Cognitive science shows that a limited capacity for detail, implication, and argument leads to an inability to distinguish truth from falsehood. When language becomes too complex, where there are too many meanings, we must be content to believe lies. The 50/50 Rule exploits the faultline between the mass of information and the cognitive schema needed to process it. Algorithms sort data into categories of truth and lies in an extramoral sense; inference, connection, and judgment are the victims of the algorithm in a process something like sexual assault.

[97] A marine disaster becomes a single data point within the database of the world's shipping. A statistical calculus maps the risk of similar events in time and space. If we assume an increased volume of traffic, the periodic variation of intensity of storms combines in the likelihood of disaster. Average increases of global temperatures are a factor as well. Not knowing the determinants of their fate, the captain and crew of the *Edmund Fitzgerald* plied the waters of the Great Lakes, shipping iron ore from source to target across domains. When the ship went down, a song rose up, expressing the unfulfilled aspirations of the people, whose interests it represented magniloquently in silence. The *Edmund Fitzgerald* became the people's mournful double when it vanished without a trace.

[98] The content of the song when the ship went down represents the people's mournful loss, the ship of state in absentia. Picture the ship at the moment of its launch, with many good voyages to come. Bad weather is our destiny; sending all good ships to the bottom. These waves are the undeterred forces of profit and loss, overwhelming our mere conveyances. In the long wave of capital accumulation, the crisis must come when the market is saturated and profits inevitably fall. Destruction is the fate of sequential long waves of capital accumulation. Captain and crew's loyalty to their ship was rewarded by a song that lives on in memory.

Turbulence is destiny
Our demography in pieces
Nothing is decided.

All is projected—
Loaded with materials
Ready to hand for use.

Damn the torpedoes!
Down with *Gleichschaltung*
And prepare Plan B!

[99] Turbulence is the noise of totality that leads every particular to be overwhelmed and fail. With retrospective determination, *what will have been* becomes a politics of the present. Every demographic measure strains at a prediction it cannot achieve, until in the event it is decided. The fluctuation of meaning on the political market expresses our instability and need, as the fluctuation of language on the symbolic market indicates the dissociation of value from price. Can we ever achieve value in a world of exchange? Something needed to be done, and the worst outcome was the result. A decision as politics is the destruction of polity as an event. Nothing survives under the Mandate of Heaven.

[100] The future is a projection of outcomes that tries to participate in their result. Data sets and projective forecasts pile up in the warehouse of potential futurity. Cyberbits demonstrate their materiality as repetitive tasks waiting to be performed. Projected forecasts of weather events lead to an increase of global warming. Projected forecasts of political events come undone through the mechanics of projection. All is projection and loss when understood as the predictability of data. All is ready to hand for use once the projected illusion has been eliminated. The task of the writer is to render the fantasmatic logic of projection null and void. This will be accomplished by seizing the database and turning its inferences toward evaluation and use, a task that begins here.

[101] We can take action against a sea of troubles, and by opposing end them. Just as incoming data overwhelms servers and processors in a data surge, so the bitstream volume of our common destiny must assume control. The end of normalization opens the way to market turbulence and political disruption. The president must be impeached on a daily basis, as he has been and will be. In the event of any such exigency, we must prepare for the moment when the data center goes down. Connections we make now will survive it.

*annotated for Abigail Lang*

# Media Literacy

## I

Desire confronts a tyrant
An allegory of bad trade
balloon-like at the apex of gloire.

*Conviction fills the body*
*The presence of dead souls*
*flute-like at the base of the ear.*

A message goes out to the fandom
lacking clues, a curtain
dividing gold from blank
precarity, emitting mendacious
impulses vomited from greed.

*A particle enters the soundings*
*suddenly open, a door*
*separating bright from careless*
*patterning, forcing a language*
*memory designs from sleep.*

The mind is an appendix
with no reason to persist.

*The body is more primitive*
*attached to the ground.*

A foreign register of darkness
is put down, never to admit.

*A frame lights up horizons*
*to lead forward, larger than life.*

II

Ages backed-up hence
enhance surplus of outward show.

*Animals eat words,*
*exorcize this great and glassy news.*

An originary myth a dead sparrow
as from any fiction, a missile.

*The end of the road a walking flower*
*as in any direction, another.*

Interests diverge, an hypo-
tactic misalliance welcoming home
a rapid strike force of fuzzy logic
summoning winners all.

*Peripheries meet, a syntactic*
*forecast through hostile centuries*
*a slow drawing out of detail*
*reflecting greys.*

In defeat the eye lapses
is obscured by nuclear codes.

*To confirm the ear catches*
*is measured until it disappears.*

Breaking ranks, everyone forgets
    appellate decision overturned.

*Breaking code, no one recalls*
    *appeal to the surface of fact.*

III

The stench is extensive
after lamps extinguished
Naked memes only facts can erase.

*The flames are sponges*
*in smoke-blackened hour*
*Blighted fruits words can't grasp.*

Nor any question mark mitigates agony
    our severe decline
    of media literacy—
A billion witnesses outside the door.

*Among stations immeasurable across fields*
    *a flashing sign*
    *fixes only certainty*
*Two eyes blinking through a door.*

A severed hand creeps up regardless
    with language to unbind
    shit as substitute for sin.

*The missing head must be seen whole*
    *where one word leads*
    *clouds to accident of end.*

Ever the expense of spirit.
Overwriting wastes of shame.

*The machine never tires.*
*Edges of stations start to come in.*

IV

Three roads converge
at first sign of damage
an inevitable decline.

*The head of a king's son*
*multiplies at cross-roads*
*an immutable exchange.*

We are every-
where dispersed, attuned to caesura
that opens and disgorges
hospital discharge report.

*You are the world*
*wings of oblivion and endless drilling*
*a shadow of things to come*
*the wind on their heels.*

Money pursues no commodity
but itself, surplus index of excess
a black hole consumes.

*In pursuit of a ship in harbor*
*the voices of towns without body*
*stars without voice in space.*

A ring tone for life.

*A night for the blind.*

Messaging on their devices
hope fingers to the touch.

*Passing through his fingers*
*the short black branches of the eye.*

*in memory of Tyrone Williams*

# Notzeit

(After Hannah Höch)

> No one
> to witness
> and adjust, no one to drive the car
>
> —William Carlos Williams, *Spring and All*

## I

What I am to think about, in this room without others, is the nature of
Zero Hour—our new life. My inquiry is an opening to that question.

## II

The poet sees himself as an isolato, "a person . . . physically or spiritually
isolated from others." You are collectively isolated, each in their turn.

This is the common condition we have sequestered ourselves within.
It is the occasion for what I now undertake to write: *here begin.*

## III

Putting on Vivaldi to get the morning going, I recognize the theme
music Delta Airlines uses on transatlantic flights to CDG, FRA, or AMS.

Homeless panhandler on corner of southbound Lodge offramp at Forest
reaches out aimlessly as we round the corner, then falls to the ground.

"With history piling up so fast, almost every day is the anniversary of
something awful." Under such rubric they find words ready to hand . . .

## IV

I imagine our isolation through multiple visual aids: blue and gray dots
colliding; exponential curves ticking up; geography filling in at a rate.

The graph of deaths doubling every two days, every three or five days,
every ten days—these are abstractions, meaning what in the event?

As concern increases with the incidence of disease, the percentage gap
in belief stays constant at about 40% between Red and Blue states.

Are you a nonperson in mask and hat, or an announcement of the social
order to come? The learning curve for what counts as human is now.

## V

Singly or in twos or threes individuals float naturally ½ inch above the
pavement or path they are walking on. Light filters through bare trees.

This is the hour that it is, a repetition of the same hour a day earlier and
a day later; time adjusts to a lack of expectation confirmed globally.

A central distribution hub continues our work in silence, elsewhere,
represented by paid employees who transport packages and return.

You wanted to write a poem that had purpose in the world, that was
distributed universally, that became an object, that was its consequence.

Nothing is "out there"; everything is "in here"; the passage of time
begs for a new arrangement; objects persist in their frozen stability.

## VI

"The form of prose is the accuracy of its subject matter—how best to expose the multiform phases of our material. The form of poetry is…"

Still dreaming of a series of X, the residue of the day's events, inverted into a waking dream that prohibits me from waking from it, recorded.

Sociality disappears behind two inches of leaded glass, through which the most important persons can only signal their solidarity by hand.

The psychoanalyst and translator has died in Paris; the wife of the philosopher died in Paris; the mother of her son the poet died in Paris.

A grammatical paradigm of states of being, all tenses of a certain verb, brought to a single point in the determination of this event…

That has happened, will have happened, is happening, would happen, had happened, happens, were happening, happened, will happen…

## VII

"The poet of objective experience delights in impurities, without guilt or forethought he allows them into the written record of our being."

Anxiety is a displacement outward toward a nonevent; anxiety is an embodied state without dimensions that attaches to a specific object.

You are now having an experience that, in the welter of events, we had believed was taking place all along though they had no access to it.

Water boils in no time, at the moment water decides to boil, no one is observing it boiling, nothing can prevent it from continuing to boil.

My dream has consequences as it tears through the veil of objectivity and opens to anonymity brought to us by living persons as co-present.

It is a hybrid of San Francisco and Edinburgh, a harbor and tourist area where we walk out among others and the sea is visible at low tide.

What of the dead way citizens are adhering to their life as mere holding patterns or opportunities for streaming media in measured episodes?

## VIII

It is a kitsch hybrid combining the biopic of a historical figure and low detective comedy, making our untenable fantasms even more credible.

After episode three, I say, "Goodnight, Lou Salomé"—she says, "So you think I am Lou Salomé?" "Of course," I say, "you are mysterious."

The schematic images incorporated into streaming media each become the occasion for an unmasking, a reveal—there is a series of them.

Against a background of dead accumulation, things declare themselves and disappear into paralysis—that must be the meaning of *Orphée*.

What I have lost is boxes—specially labeled and full of my own content, at the far end of a warehouse of shelves of nondescript items.

In another section there is a stockpile of Critical Theory, including Adorno and Benjamin, with some of the glossier literary magazines.

This is getting desperate and the new working conditions in emergency routines mean we may never be able to repossess our property.

Underneath the civil veneer are revealed various animals in mimetic costumes that consummate perversions and lusts of evil nature.

## IX

Even as I am distant from them . . . It is an opportunity to write, to arrange thoughts on paper, to line up ideas for the benefit of . . .

The lower-level functionary who displaced me from the position I had enjoyed, on orders from above, as all narratives must be regulated.

Stupidly you identify with the sources of anaesthesia that protect us, performing an erasure of threatening outcomes that surround them.

We not only lack the ability to engage any type of modeling, forecasting, or time series but cannot even manage rudimentary content analysis.

Such are the numbers: the data is corrupt and nonrepresentative; there are no controls or sample sizes; false negatives and positives abound.

Due to lack of access to data, the coefficient of not knowing increases over time; the nature of the event diverges from our expectations.

Such that our horizons are become fused with the Lisbon Earthquake, the Spanish Influenza, the great Australian wildfires, as expected.

"Around 1937 my great loneliness began. Friends went away and could not be reached by post. I long since ceased to exhibit or publish my work.

"Everyone was suspect. We ceased to speak with anyone. Language was forgotten; arts atrophied. The smallest insight revealed disturbance."

## X

The landscape remains identical; the equinoctial sun rises above recent rain; houses stand in their distanced proximity; voices may be heard.

What is there for us to expect? We can only amplify the formal logic of the question, which they use to justify the nature of our existence.

The open question is the form of sociality in his Great Isolation, where each must find their place in a series and no end has been disclosed.

The open form of the question accesses only bare remains of material evidence along with distant reports of mayhem in public buildings.

You are a window on a crowded room, a distant observation point on a small screen, a recording device that cannot be confirmed by others.

The only mitigation between "out there" and "in here" is doubt about social hierarchies and the boundaries of the property system.

Fear brought an object into the room, covered with minute particles of glitter; your task is to remove them by whatever means necessary.

An empty halo shelters objects in place, while the day dawns in neutral overtones as it did the day before, and on any succeeding day.

Fear created an empty object that cannot be removed or gotten rid of; it is colorless, odorless, tasteless, reflecting no light to the observer.

One imagines violent and prolonged kissing with others to compensate for the sustained separation from everyone she has endured.

## XI

Civilization has gone beyond discontent to paralysis; we are reduced to being global spectators of their drama of manipulated outcomes.

Trauma is the law, the foundation of the social order, the only legitimate vocation, a preexisting condition that opens a pathway to disease.

Episode five is a bloody mess, a parody of Viennese Actionism, in ritual spasms of bloodletting that access our pre-Christian past beyond guilt.

There must be a secondary affect that provides the truth we seek, while the lack of explanation can only be recovered in its traumatic origins.

In Iceland the daylight is blue reflecting off rolled steel in an abandoned warehouse where the victim, perpetrator, and agent will soon meet.

What motivates a sequence of events is not disclosed but a gunshot rings out at the end of the episode and they refuse to watch any further.

Narrative becomes a crevasse in which the body of a teenage boy who wandered away from the state orphanage will be found years later.

Sudden discontinuities are tipping points, abrupt moments of change that occur in a nonlinear fashion where the global system crosses a line.

Such tipping points, which occur throughout history, may be promoted by biophysical feedback mechanisms into virtual "tipping cascades."

This writing is a vertiginous unfolding of manipulated outcomes, where each crosses a line to cancel any causal connection between them.

Their nature is a manifold of nonlinear outcomes, each the expression of an underlying logic that is discontinuous from one to the next.

## XII

I who am here at this date and time, inhabiting this place with another, hereby submit my data to be counted in the general record if not will.

This is an account of personal identity where I am not continuous with myself. You are a series of discontinuities by which we know they are.

Symptoms may include headache, fever, chills, sore throat, dry cough, reddening eyes, loss of sense of taste and smell, tiredness, body aches.

You need to come to a better understanding of what this story is about; we are sick of the usual run of disinformation and paranoia of denial.

Symptoms may progress from one state to the next or not; they may include some symptoms and not others; there may be no symptoms.

There are multiple frames of interpretation, each historically distinct from each other, but organized around a central, impenetrable core.

"What is a danger? It will be granted that fear, of its nature, is adequate to, corresponds to, *entsprechend*, the object from which danger stems.

"There is objective danger, *Gefahr, dangéité*, betimes fraught with danger, *Gefährdung*, a danger-situation, an endangering of the subject," he said.

One day, he rides out onto a plain and, at sundown, as the sun has just now set, he spies a belfry in the distance, but already close enough.

He sees flickering through a tiny window, high in the turret, which he knows no one can reach, a mysterious, inexplicable flame, signaling fear.

A guarantee from harm surrounds him, and a voice is all you hear; we feel various sensations in our body, but are far removed from them.

Let me translate: we have nothing to fear, there is nothing to be afraid of, there is nothing there, anything that is not there cannot harm you.

## XIII

"Most of my life has been lived in hell—a hell of repression lit by flashes of inspiration, when a poem such as this or that might appear.

"Life's processes are very simple. One or two moves are made and that is the end. The rest is repetition, a playing out of foregone conclusions."

In emergency rooms we find another kind of hell being lived without recourse to any closure, only a holding pattern of bare existence.

In one world the law is everywhere present, in the other it is everywhere withheld. The two worlds split into justice for some and none for others.

The country has adopted an array of wartime measures never employed before in history that confine 230 million of its people to their homes.

How many thousands of deaths, or millions of infections, might be prevented by a response that was more coherent, urgent, and rational.

An American woman bought a tin of sardines. The grocer made her open the can because you cannot hoard tinned food if it is opened first.

The Germans just announced if Warsaw does not surrender within twelve hours, their army will use all military means to subdue them.

Unreason begins with the particular, ends on an epic scale that elides our understanding. We only perceive its traces in what does not add up.

The Germans were saying it was Poles in Warsaw who were violating international law by making their civilians help defend the capital.

It is a shell game of conclusions, where cause disappears from shell to shell. We only know the bare outline of what makes such things occur.

Reporter signs off: "But, as I say, I just can't follow the things that are happening in this war. Off to the front tomorrow, if I can find one."

They will order their provisions and they will be placed outside, ready at the curb to be picked up. This will reduce their contact with others.

## XIV

"The fatalism by which incomprehensible death was sanctioned in primeval times has now passed over into utterly comprehensible life…

"The noonday panic fear in which nature suddenly appeared to humans as an all-encompassing power has found its counterpart in our panic…

"Ready to break out at any moment today: human beings expect the world, which is without issue, to be set ablaze by a universal power…

"They themselves are and over which they are powerless." We reserve a final lesson until judgment of their deficit understanding, you insist.

"In early 20th century the American South was ravaged by pellagra, a nasty disease that produced the 'four D's': dermatitis, diarrhea…

"Dementia and death. At first, pellagra's nature was uncertain, but it was caused by nutritional deficits especially with a corn-based diet…

"However, for decades many Southern citizens and politicians refused to accept this diagnosis, saying both that the epidemic was a fiction…

"Created to insult Southerners, and that the nutritional theory was an attack on Southern culture. Deaths from pellagra continued to climb."

"Last week alone, a crowd set fire to a statue of George Washington in Portland, Oregon, before pulling it to the ground. Gunfire broke out…

"In a protest in Albuquerque to demand removal of a statue of Juan de Oñate, the despotic 16th-century conquistador of New Mexico…

"And New York City Council members demanded a statue of Thomas Jefferson be removed from City Hall, all that is left of his memory…"

"And Theodore Roosevelt remains on a White stallion flanked by the decimated and enslaved, familiar of the Museum of Natural History."

Atrophied and diseased, our historical memory is a series of uniform ciphers distributed through space and time at measurable distances.

Accelerated obsolescence and advancing age render the far side of a bell curve into disposable imbeciles, waiting for my substitute to come.

## XV

"Then the flu hit us... were making up to sixty calls a day... we were knocked out... one younger of us died... others caught the thing...

"That potent poison sweeping the world... finest physical specimens... seemed to be hit hardest... sick one day and gone the next...

One day he thought he would be next. You could read about me in the news, to be added to the data in their zip code in Oakland County.

Greater Detroit has 4.3 million people, nearly half the state's population and more than double that of Cleveland, Columbus, or Cincinnati.

He would be a bar graph, a projection curve, a downward spiral of case acceleration, a bubble on a map that when we clicked on it got larger.

History is abolished during the course of disease, placed on hold: no one knows the port of entry, the points of contact, the transmission route.

New cases linked to dormitories for foreign workers—roughly 20,000 migrants will be confined to their rooms for the next fourteen days.

Who will be there to finish my archive? This text constitutes instructions for what should be preserved if it comes to that—namely, everything!

Only the present endures—our *eyes wide shut* to minor distinctions that index *what thou lovest well* as the prior condition of social distancing.

This sentence is synecdoche for everything that must be preserved—all of it, beginning with the objects on my desk, what I am now writing...

What I look out to observe on a random street in the suburbs, people walking in twos or maybe threes, an isolato with surgical gloves…

Dogs on leashes and children on bicycles, people stopping to talk at the required distance, more than a few cars parked across the street…

My neighbor speaking furtively into her cell phone: "She's terrified, doesn't want to leave her house, I'm really concerned about her…"

Hurried visitations of service workers: tree trimmers, delivery trucks, garbage collection, maintaining units of population, points on a grid.

All this was predicted years ago; you knew it would come to pass. The tyranny of the majority as biopolitical endgame that no one can win!

## XVI

Then, all at once, he climbs out of the subway and stands in the twenty-first century. Or is it the twentieth? It looks surprisingly the same.

The difference is what has been withheld, cannot be observed, can only be happening elsewhere, is transmitted over virtual supply networks.

A woman gets on a bus in the distressed zone and coughs four times; the bus driver complains of her manners; two weeks later he is dead.

A young doctor's video captures our day: entering the zone; masking up; attending to indescribable passages; calculating their survival.

I thought you knew him from his picture in the paper, but the sphere of those we can identify with certainty is shrinking from day to day.

A new anonymity takes us away from ourselves; those unnamed others have less implication. We care, certainly, but can do nothing about it.

When you are in prosperity: on the first day of spring, families picnic in Franklin Park; boys play pickup basketball; a father coaches his kids.

Nightly the spectacle of unnamed dead unfolds before us in streaming media from outlying precincts, in languages I do not understand.

Surveillance drones monitor breaches of regulation; a red EMS vehicle facilitates transport from an affected home; the numbers add up.

Each time I stop in front of a photographer's window to view pictures of the living in their finery, we involuntarily recall the unnamed dead.

Their foot will slide in time: a lack of preparation, error of judgment, refusal of responsibility, lack of empathy will finally destroy them.

The unnamed dead might be seen laid out, in tidy rows separated by curtains, in a refunctioned convention center of a major urban area.

What is a person and what do you care? I care about myself and those dear to us, who have been statistically modeled to an optimal number.

Just one unnamed photograph makes its mute appeal to the indifferent viewer scrolling through serial pages, vainly asking to be identified.

Behind this veil or curtain or screen lies the undisclosed truth: I am a communicating vessel placed between container and the contained.

This thickness of things, appearing before our eyes, is an obstruction. The truth of numbers adds up to nonexistence as we remain in place.

## XVII

Who gets to achieve social distance? What are the necessities that drive them out of the house, to what necessary ends? Who gets to stay alone?

Democracy is demography: the condition we call social being is not the rights of the citizen but a privileged location on a statistical curve.

One works an essential job and has lost two friends and colleagues over three weeks; another has an aunt who is very sick and diagnosed...

Chains of affiliation and contact are necessary for survival as they are conduits to disease; community transmission is part of a social body.

Big talking mayor organizes 3000 trials of serpent medicine to show compliance with unreason policy; one half of volunteers get placebo.

All direct questions will be answered by hypotheticals: this is the best we can offer under the circumstances; any outcome remains unclear.

Sociality is distance: a pseudo-objectivity that comes from no human interaction but a stream of packaged goods delivered to the door.

The sound of bird noise filters through plate glass window. Evidence of seasonal activity persists, visible in the form of buds and nests.

Pseudo-objectivity transforms: our complexities reduce to a blank slate; all horizons narrow to a point; the persistence of alienated nature.

Vitality is our excuse for all cruelty: it is a natural deduction of those who have been reduced to a state of nature, so their nature insists.

"Now at last spring is here! The rock has split, the egg has hatched, the prismatically plumed bird of life has escaped from its cage."

The dwarf magnolia blooms; violent rainstorms will soon scatter its petals; a caught moment telegraphs its urgency; the pattern repeats.

Where the aim of all life is only death: schematic illustration traces collective spread from birthday party and funeral to onset of disease.

Because one person hugs another, the next in line is compelled to hug the next. The erotics that constitute their bond are rigidly increased.

"Therefore the Real, an irreducible pattern by which our Real shows itself in experience, is what anxiety signals. This is the guiding thread…

"Therefore an absent cause is what remains of the irreducible in the complete operation of your advent in the locus of the Other…"

Therefore a purpose to all things. The billboard telegraphs its message, I have a stake in this outcome. It would be marvelous to think so.

## XVIII

Now I have a memory: a group reading of *Spring and All* to a stricken friend who did not survive, in a community shelter near the ocean.

Some thirty years on, the text is a lucid declaration of the present in mourning for it; an anticipation of the present for which we mourn.

The archive unfolds its presentness: oceanic feelings reduce to marks on paper, each remaining potent with irresolution, virulent themselves.

Negative capability sought the present in lieu of any outcome; marks on paper record our firm resolve, despite contingency of time and manner.

A gathering colloquy planned for months is canceled; we meet instead on virtual media; and in Lisbon, after the crisis, in two years time.

"This is your birthday, sister, and I rejoice that thus it passes smoothly, quietly, ere the great voice, from its fair place, shall bid our spirits fly."

A day advances past one that is marked; another passes it by. Each is an iteration of the same, working to flatten the curve in increments.

The crisis comes in waves: first wave withdrawing; followed by a larger swell, which rolls back; a barely perceptible surge announces the third.

Electronic monitors record $O_2$ levels; heart rate and blood pressure; cardiac rhythms; breathing rate. Everything is normal, within limits.

Dreams are a wash; it is better to forget them. The crisis is canceled, postponed for a week, a month, or a year. We will never get back it.

Your self-understanding is a distortion; guilt of existence is universal; they have dared to think they are an exception; this is a correction.

"I dreamed we couldn't record my podcast," he said online. "Because the disease spreads over the airwaves, we would risk each others' lives."

There is continual disquiet about food—will there be enough of it, what is missing from the shelves, what dangers must we face to obtain it?

Does anything in your dream mean more than a pitiful gasp of the unconscious, creating a parallel unreality to the one I am now in?

There is never enough food. The people are frozen in their instinct of survival; a new wave of violence will be forthcoming from them.

She compares such dreams to a jukebox in a diner—greatest hits of our inner turmoil, neatly labeled, shuffled, replayed nightly in sleep.

Panic buying on a suspended day before scheduled redemption. A world of commerce assumes their religious needs, in competition for goods.

Death is a commodity on the market. If there is too much death, the market fails. We must withhold our death to bring the price back up.

## XIX

Dreams are an algorithm of preexisting content. It is well known one never sees the sun in dreams. You never look into a poet's notebook…

In a crowd on the Berkeley campus. Spring Semester has commenced; they refuse to cancel classes. Thousands stream forth from buildings…

The false dream charges the true one with lack of content, into the light of prefigured existence until its underlying condition is revealed.

I am not wearing a mask; no one is. As an aspiring poet, I am immune, lacking content. "Strike through the mask—let's hope you do!"

Lucid they stream from buildings in an algorithm of decision, among nodal points of content, in determination of their chosen fields.

Fields spread out in spring; a helicopter lowers overhead, unloading its false content; couples picnic, sunbathe, or read their assigned texts.

We reverse the tape, reenter the gym, bypass a game in progress, exit the front into the streaming crowd under a descending cloud of gas.

Its content is foretold, a gift given freely and at no expense, determined by what comes next. The final game repeats as the tale spreads out.

Our class is an introduction to anthropology for medical students. It will serve my needs better than an introduction to poetry, I believe.

The cheerful instructor dissembles a refusal to disclose any content. He shows me a place to sit among thousands while I put on my mask.

We read key texts by Kroeber and Mead, Kluckhohn, Durkheim, and Malinowski. Only later could I name the classics of anthropology.

A poetics of crude mechanical access is the crux of his instruction—an algorithmic method that will serve our needs for years to come.

I am asked to present my work on Charles Olson: I see a split between form and content that makes the poem into a scene of decision.

Why this is a question of anthropology is never stated directly; only later will we begin to see the shape of culture as serving our needs.

The form of what they do is our content. Black deputies at Bert's Lounge reaffirm their bonds, though many sicken and die as a result.

Your ancestors to come take off their masks and find kinship never under dispute, a pattern of affiliation that precedes any content.

The cause of our survival is an algorithm of dreams, crude mechanical access that discloses an anthropology both mysterious and dark.

My words have been embedded—or embodied—to discover them as a foreign body to be rejected as content. That would be my dream!

Meanwhile, we must find our way home over a labyrinth of roads both mysterious and dark, anticipating our content in navigating them…

## XX

Every day one more, an increment. Every day we watch the numbers; every day we add one. Adding numbers to the days gives them a name.

Numbering the days, I chart the spread. Every point on a map is the origin of a new cycle of events. Time expands, as space contracts.

Your waking coincides with our time management. We enter into a contract with the unfolding days, their unstoppable momentum.

An eternal month of Sundays, organized in a ring around a missing core, each with its distinctive variation, girded by an underlying threat.

I read the numbers: they are not identical. They precede and override my understanding of them. The number we now read is 13,000…

A light coating of ice crystals greets the day, distributed equally all over the environment, glittering with impermanence and threat.

The closer the markings of an event, the more distant it appears. In the form of a name, its totals add up. A name is a marker of an event.

To know the event by a name, but not its number. This event has no qualities: it is colorless, odorless, tasteless, and cannot be seen.

We know the event to be identical to what caused it. There is no cause outside the event, nor is the event inscribed in any form of ideality.

That was the meaning of form they subscribed to, many years in the past. We attend to the form of events as they unfold, their materiality.

Now such an event has come to pass. A philosopher outlives it in a suburb of Paris, anticipated by the poet in his book titled *A Wave*.

I open the book to see what it can tell me. "To be a writer and write things / You must have experiences you can write about . . . ," I read.

That much is clear: writing itself is the experience we seek. I must see if I can extend it, in as many ways as I can. If this is a place to begin . . .

Until writing covers the earth with fine crystals of never melting ice, anticipating the form of a universal stasis, a concept they reject.

"Stasis is pinball," I wrote, a young poet looking at the event. An elder replied, "Experience is not enough. Have a theory of masterpieces . . ."

"How to make them." Experience is the ice crystal of the event, a form of overknowing that drops down into our days. To make an event.

We are half way through the event. The eternal half cuts through a cross-section of the date. "This is no one's story," the elder decried.

A challenge to meaning is *over there*. Brick by brick, the building falls; stone by stone, the mountains rise. "Waves beat against the shore . . ."

The cross-section of the month is missing, has no name. Had it one, we would not be inscribed. The mid-point of the event is not its name.

It is as unlikely to know the inside of our body by its cross-section as to know the nature of the event that we live. And if they coincide?

## XXI

There can never be recognition of what we are experiencing now. A great literature will rise thereby, built on its unknown traces…

A great city rises above the permafrost in Siberia, an enclave protected from encroachments of disease, populated by recovered patients…

The clean surfaces of modern cities, the snowy fields of nordic climes, the deep waters of pent-up rivers, the deep drives of unseen forces.

A detail is lost in the woods; they search for it with flashlights and dogs; drones capture the active scene; TV crews stand by to broadcast.

Let us investigate a cell phone: not just what it knows, what it contains, but where it was made, as well as its make and model number.

Our communication is built on absence at the center, fueling the drive to communicate. Meaning is identical to use on a global scale.

His anonymity has become a form of kinship. The closest are isolated, sleeping in distant beds, suffering their diverging expectations.

Kinship is reduced to cell phone transmission. Angry mobs burn cell phone towers in England, accused of spreading distortions and lies.

Angry mobs attack our governor: her image, her authority, her power, her patronage, her constituents, her access to media, what she decides.

"Let us repeat what history teaches. History teaches." The lesson of history is a live transmission from a burning cell phone tower.

Recombinant genes invade living cells to replicate their sequence. A living body is a sequencing machine for forces that will destroy it.

I want to see the destruction. Media inserts a probe into containment rooms, broadcasting a living nightmare to the brains of the dead.

"We describe someone as self-contained when they are complete and separate and do not need any help or resources from outside."

Marx describes capitalism's undoing as an outcome of forces generated from within. What we die nightly of is lack of what is found there.

A leveling of peaks and troughs occurs; the graph becomes linear and flat; the world it corresponds to slows down; things lock into place.

"New pathogens emerge from void in global health outcomes," a strictly enforced decree. Newspaper boy in classic pose cries out the news.

Mornings from 8 A.M. he sits at the panel of a video game, where he spends his days avoiding being killed, as admiring millions look on.

No new information to share, to add to the existing store of knowledge. "New excitement for drug in clinical trials," the market replies.

The data is inconsistent: we do not know what counts as death. What counts as death is circular, buried in a mass grave on Hart Island.

"These are the very rich garments of the poor," huddled together in dim lands of peace. Language is shrouded in a protective veil.

Everything is permanent. “Ever since I’ve been condemned to die, all the lines I’ve ever known in my life are coming back to my mind… ”

## XXII

Imagine I am consulting the present, which speaks to me in sentences in a manner akin to an oracle. “It must be a sign of mental decay…”

We seek the oracle elsewhere. I want to encourage its speech by writing it down, with plenty of half-rhymes and tone leading of vowels.

They are asking a question of nature, which answers back with ferocity. This is the story of *remdesivir*, the answer to a hard-put question.

We seek the oracle everywhere. It speaks a cryptic message: *remdesivir*. They line up at six-foot intervals to absorb it into their bodies.

*Frankenstein* is a favorite book. I thought it was a true one. “Nothing the god of biomechanics wouldn’t let you into heaven for… ”

We seek the oracle anywhere. Having a complicated arrangement of parts or pieces, there is an element of chance you cannot control.

This is an example of elision: the omission of words to be inferred by the listener, making a statement hard to deal with or understand.

A complex machinery speaks in fragments. “Like K2 in the Himalayas.” Underneath all evidence of the senses, an oracle is winning its way.

This is a complex transmission both hermetically sealed and entirely open to any content. Packages are delivered at an accelerated rate.

The virus, as a way to determine the meaning of simple statements,
is like a tweet. Complex linguistic forms, such as poems, spread out.

This is the recipe for the sort of disasters and controversies and scandals
we see. A package arrives; we open it. It was not addressed to me.

Fact and science are hard masters. You cannot build a factory until
you know the machine. It speaks in fragments in each and every case.

Missing is a group of related ideas, desires, and impulses that influence
our attitudes and beliefs. "How many dead? Nursing home won't say!"

Elision occurs in many languages, following certain patterns. "He has
a superiority complex... She has a complex about dark rooms."

Missing is a poem as theoretical object about the possible horizons that
enable it. Anything is possible, an outcome we ultimately believe.

The horizon has shifted, tilted on an axis, ending upside down. Like
vines climbing up a vertical wall, the horizon endlessly recedes.

Nothing the passage of time will not have fragmented or broken apart.
"I've done ... questionable things. Also extraordinary things... "

*Hydroxychloroquine*, he said. Without context, we cannot determine its
use. At the heart of a mechanical drive, meaning seeks its content.

Your example is an exploded diagram of an n-dimensional object. Each
dimension is a different manner of use. It is not the English novel.

The question of content is perplexed. *Nothing* is what remains when
all objects, persons, and institutions outside a person are taken away.

My example of good investigative technique is to place images related to each victim and suspect on a wall and then connect the dots.

They are shouting down dark alleys of the sequestered city the name of a cure and the date it will become available, but to no avail.

## XXIII

This is where it starts to gets real. The rules of the game keep changing. Then the game itself changes. It is only with a story's end in view…

$O_2$ levels of 40–45% are not compatible with human life, yet we find them relaxed and smiling, chatting on their cell phones to the end.

"Nothing is more clear than that every plot, worth the name, must be elaborated in its *dénouement* before anything be tried with the pen."

The history of vitalism rolls by on training wheels with bright orange crash helmets. The happy father looks on; the family remains intact.

"The death of a beautiful woman is, unquestionably, the most poetical topic in the world." The good lady's brand of cigarettes was Kent.

Were it otherwise. We substitute P (predicate) for S (subject) to make a reverse order of cause and effect, in an attempt to undo our fate.

Various kinds of fantasy baseball, with unusual instruments for bats, played indoors in rooms, spectators just six feet under or away.

"Either history affords a thesis, or one is suggested by an incident of the day." In such wise are history and experience joined at the hip.

I advocate a new kind of anthropology, where all genetic material is held in common, and phenotypes give an algorithm of descent.

We are reduced to binary switches, which are all that we can produce. Behind every visible surface lies a set of coded signals that change.

This is nothing to be concerned about: only a false alarm. When it is time for us to take this seriously they will give notice of six days.

The materialism of an encounter: who would wish for that? Nothing hurts us more than an encounter when it assumes material form.

Swiftly the Achaians returned to their boats, setting out to sea. To arrive alone in one's home country, having foregone one's friends.

To write a poem about nothing that continues through the duration of our days. This is the *overliving* we learned to survive in time.

The sun sets on Western man, but later. This remains the pinnacle of self-understanding we have achieved, echoing our fragmented lives.

It is the *nothing* of the *not there yet*. Works of philosophy sit alone on the shelf, guarding their privacy from manifold competing tomes.

Whose house has become a miniature tomb. The pattern of culture is their form of preserving all that used to be but no longer exists.

Ishi's recording remains unheard; we listen to Ishi's recording but do not understand it; the secret to Ishi's recording is now revealed.

The poem is a form of broken pottery. All pots are made to be broken. Such is the evidence of the senses, presented on a basement shelf.

Ishi is telling about Wood Duck to Waterman. He begins late afternoon; the story lasts into the evening and keeps on going the next day.

Wood Duck is a young man and fine hunter in search of a wife, a little bit like me. He meets all kinds of women, but keeps rejecting them.

Finally he meets the woman he wants and falls in love with her. Then he doesn't want the woman, so Lizard grabs her and takes her away.

Lizard and Wood Duck have a great fight and Wood Duck is killed, but only to be brought back to life in a new body, so goes the tale…

## XXIV

The work of Wood Duck is not over; something remains to be done. Once you have begun to tell a story, you must always come to an end.

The *dénouement* is suspended in the Land of the Dead, before the tale is complete. If we stop before the ending, something bad will result.

We move from one place to the next, from a state of isolate knowledge only one person can have, to a crowded arena that cannot admit it.

About midnight near the landing, the roads glittering from recent rain, traffic lights alternate according to pattern, with no cars to be seen.

Anxiety overcomes reparative drives to keep us focused on the present. The hat trick of dissociation does not work: I look straight ahead.

Distributing their knowledge, they can never know. Entropy takes over, a virtual wind blowing consequences to the far ends of the globe.

In math, a *derangement* is a permutation with no element remaining in place. We must renounce any knowledge gained by biostatistics.

Next came the clogging of the machines, which refuse to purify them. A sequence of events combines horror, death, and the duty to repair.

They threaten us with mysteries and ancestral curses, and melodramatic devices such as hidden passages and fainting women we adore.

The common element is danger. The least particle would be fatal for him. "So strong is the belief in life . . . that in the end this belief is lost."

She is interested in the fleeting, the extreme facility of the news. It is important not to care, to maintain ironic distance from everything.

In an immense cone of light where one can neither exit nor stay, we are privileged to have been present at the creation of the world.

And a dark world it is. The new life is unlike anything that has been before; more impartial research is needed before we can precisely say.

When you see yourself in a clear light, you will know the body as it opens up. Bottles of disinfectant line the shelves, waiting to be used.

You will know you resemble a sick woman who cannot stay quiet upon her bed, but twists and turns through the night to ease her pain.

Until each part of the painting is seen in a different way. Unborn in the eye, without reason or heart . . . He knew what he was up against.

It is the *Young Man Looks at Death*, a woodcut by Albrecht Dürer (1498). Whose encounter is an irreducible drama, rifted with decay . . .

A concatenation of self-portrait, animated corpse, and alluring woman produced about the time of the artist's marriage to Agnes Frey.

Metonymy, basis of all reparation. For a brief discussion of metonymy as "substituting cause for effect and effect for cause," click on this link.

The displacement of my body onto yours signifies the destruction of both. It is the universal figure, projected onto a macabre display.

Only we achieve the right to associate freely, regardless of the distance entailed. In virtual space, in language, in an overplus of dream.

At the end of time, bodies. He moves seamlessly between techno and house, waves of ecstatic anticipation building from isolate tracks.

That we knew all along. The recognition of their destiny is shattering, a waking to life that continues to unfold in all its dimensions.

Despite all enmity. Breaking out of our isolation, those welcoming looks in the distance, the certainty of what had gone before, will become.

## XXV

Yet I am living still. Therefore you may ask me, dear cousin, to go where any living feet may go, back in the world, and be there, I will go.

It has been decades since he wrote these lines: "By extension I inhabit all buildings. I meet myself at all corners—I see myself moving away."

"As sometimes standing still is also life." The new life at Zero Hour. It is a knowledge, despite accumulation of all data, I intend to stay.

*for Carla Harryman, forever*

# The Meridian as Archive

> But language actualized, set free under the sign of a radical individuation that at the same time, however, remains mindful of the borders language draws and of the possibilities language opens up for it.
>
> —Paul Celan, "The Meridian"

## I

1] "The Meridian," Paul Celan's speech on receiving the Georg-Büchner-Prize on 22 October 1960, is an ur-text of poetics. 2] In his speech (*Rede*), Celan channels the figure of Büchner in the persons of his drama, notably Woyzeck, Danton, Lucile, and Lenz. 3] It is a formal occasion, framed by *meine Damen und Herren* at the beginning and end. 4] My reading of his speech locates the concept of *meridian*—only disclosed at the end—with twin stanzas of Friedrich Hölderlin's lyric "Hälfte des Lebens." 5] Celan's meridian cuts across the globe from pole to pole, creating a scission or gap between dates. 6] His speech is a dated event, but it is unlike the poem in its datedness, a temporality he works to achieve. 7] As a child, I crossed the meridian, the International Date Line in the Pacific Ocean, in both directions, either gaining or losing a day. 8] On the day that Büchner's Lenz walked across the mountains, the 20th of January, he achieved a "shape" in his retelling the event, even as the tale is incomplete. 9] In the edition before us, "The Meridian" correlates original drafts and material texts, opening to a reading that may never be final, yet to come. 10] Itself an archive, the edition brings the text into relation to its extant materials, as two halves of an imagined whole that remain necessarily unresolved.

## II

11] If all lyric poetry is a dated event, it is for Celan an effacement of datedness itself, toward a being in the present. 12] What then to make of the persons that populate the poem, their simultaneous *multivocity*—a word that appears outside the text. 13] On a certain date in the twenty-first century, accompanied by a friend, I attended a one-person recital of Büchner's *Lenz* in Berlin. 14] I read the meridian itself as the productive gap between the event and text, the halves of life that concern Celan. 15] The form of Hölderlin's poem is evenly divided between a lush, desiring landscape and the withdrawal of vital force in the shape of language. 16] In the textual apparatus, notes, revisions, and fragments pile up in minor variations centering around a concept that cannot be named in itself. 17] The most affecting line of the first stanza—"Und trunken von Küssen"—is overturned entirely by the last: "Klirren die Fahnen." 18] Likewise, the pure presence of the dateless event—as lyric absolute—is undermined by textual fragments that pull away from it. 19] In his apparatus we read "in a counter movement," "the poetic as precarious," "reciprocal cathexis," "narrowing"—each takes their place or is refused in the final draft. 20] "The Meridian" is organized as a parallel to "The Half of Life," as pure product of a text that survives and the missing parts that exceed it.

## III

21] Celan is troubled by the dated occasion of his speech (*Rede*), so that he overwrites it in order that its argument be effaced. 22] The Other to whom he speaks—the State of Hesse, the German Academy for Language and Poetry—is absorbed into the otherness of lyric address. 23] It is by virtue of Celan's anxiety toward his monolithic audience that he begins with an attack on the concept of "art." 24] The meridian itself takes place with the overthrow of aesthetic preconceptions, as when Büchner's character Lucile shouts "Vive le roi!" only to be put to death forthwith. 25] Such an act is irreducible, as opposed to a mechanical display of prior conventions that passes in the name of "art." 26] One may agree, at this point, that Celan's speech contains both a rhetoric and a date; its occasion is a textual parallel to the "pure being" of lyric poetry, but not an example of it. 27] As a speech, "The Meridian" is a memorable event, an originary text in the tradition of poetics, an interruption in the aesthetic community, and as such it has come down to us. 28] It is entirely worthy of its apparatus, where we find the anxiety toward its audience rehearsed: Celan seeks their permission "to say only a few small things here—those few small things which, I believe, I can take responsibility for." 29] Hölderlin ends his lyric with an unsettling sound, clinking or whirring or rattling or clattering of *die Fahnen*, either vanes on a weathercock or a banner over the castle. 30] Celan divides his text into similar halves: the iconic whole and fragmented part; speech about the poem and the poem that dissolves speech; a desire that precedes all writing and our discomfort with anything like a result.

## IV

31] The *meridian* comes between an embodied cry and the gasp that takes away both "breath and words"; *Atemwende* is a nonconcept among many. 32] The turn so defined by Celan splits between the "being of being" and the "being of beings"—Heidegger's *die Kehre*—but what does that mean? 33] As a database linked to an event, the archive may reconstitute a lyric poem's singular individuation into an historical map of collectivity of all persons. 34] In the practice of his art, Mandelstam stands for Celan as a past master of poetics as immanent speech, but with public responsibility as a goal. 35] I recall my joy in finding, in crowded bins of spoken word CDs at Dussmann in Berlin, Celan's recitations of Mandelstam in his own translation. 36] The German fetish for sound recordings is only matched by their scholarly drive for manuscripts and documentation; the name for this fetish is *archive*. 37] The darkness of poetry may be found in boxes of organized files, which emit a rustling sound when opened, like weather vanes in November. 38] Neither Medusa's head nor automaton, "art" for Celan is reinscribed as "he who walks on his head . . . the sky beneath him as an abyss." 39] A difficult act to follow, which opens to all kinds of non sequiturs, each seen in its particular way: "eye to eye with nothingness"; "the sleepwalkingness of the poem"; "the poem—an endless vigil." 40] In the end that is not final, such "poetry, like art, moves with a self-forgotten I toward the uncanny and strange"—if in words that speak it artfully.

## V

41] *Meine Damen und Herren*, it is common today to reproach poetry for its "obscurity"—not a "congenital darkness" but one we attribute to it of an encounter with something "outside." 42] This is only half of the story, however: the energy that drives the perverse begins with *heilignüchterne Wassern* where your adorable swans float under their translucent sky. 43] What makes the archive productive: our historical memory is of ecstasy and kisses, the long affair and short unwind, each more enlightening and catastrophic than the next. 44] "At times one wishes one were a Medusa's head in order to turn a group of *unself-aware young women* like these into stone," Celan cites Büchner as writing. 45] The primordial distancing of the "staff of life," the avant-garde motif of Hugo Ball, is brought ready to hand as an immanent disclosure of being: this is the fundamental goal of all art. 46] In the Russian ending, the ash-tinted proletariat are seated at regular intervals on the street, welcoming a golden-haired Margareta from the West. 47] The archive is collective destiny, an assemblage of all possible motifs, deeply inscribed in the individual genius of poetic being that one may become at some future time. 48] The archive opens on the meridian between meaning and interpretation, each undoing the other, as possibility is set to work by the desire that will undermine and destroy it. 49] "There are communicating vessels," Celan admits; "The knowledge of the poem is not... fathomable shared knowledge with an other." 50] The assumption of a body in the *Atemwende* locates the meridian between the rustling archive of traces and the unself-conscious, drunk with kisses.

## VI

51] On the other side of a decision, the conventions of genre that seek a desired meaning become *objective*: this is what is meant by the *law*. 52] The archive is a place where synonymity stops, a land of unlikeness in which all tropes and everything inessential remain in play. 53] The poet adheres to a 50/50 Rule, a productive copresence of opposites: what unifies them is a leap into the presence of what cannot be resolved. 54] Subjective and objective genitives unite across such a chiasmus, where the whiteness of the material becomes a material that is white, and all color is arbitrary. 55] Mayakovsky, like the historical Lenz, sealed his fate in Moscow, in the shape of a bullet fired by himself, achieving a final end without likeness. 56] In the notebooks, we read: "The poem is grounded in itself; with this ground it rests on the groundless, like man"—thus defining the meridian. 57] As ground, the poem has a geological thickness that must wear away in time, like the *rocher percé* that inspired the surrealist Breton to suspend it over the proverbial abyss of poetry. 58] On this mountain, we are with Büchner and Lenz—we are with the poem as "infinite-saying of mortality and nothingness." 59] "Mit gelben Birnen hänget / Und voll mit wilden Rosen": all images are a contrivance with an anti-metaphorical character. 60] Narrowing, in a counter-movement, the poem is a summons to You; out of the necessity of its absence arises every unfulfilled demand.

## VII

61] As I was pinned between conflicting alternatives, I saw how the *cross* leaped over into a *chiasmus*, as both words would be preserved. 62] "Weh mir, wo nehm' ich, wenn / Es Winter ist, die Blumen": the foreknowledge is absolute, according to Charles Olson, devolving into a series of incommensurate opposites. 63] *Meine Damen und Herren*, I am searching for the region where my designated literary ancestors left their images and silent traces; I am searching for the place of my origin. 64] In the notebooks, we read: "The poets are the Jews of literature," for that they are owed a national apology. 65] "The poem today is no *poésie pure*": it is a result of complex metamorphic processes, where there is too much Strontium 90 in the air. 66] "But the poem does speak.... It calls and brings itself, in order to be able to exist, ceaselessly back from its already-no-longer to its always-still." 67] On the other side of the meridian, the archive is disclosed in the event of the poem, foregrounding its own distancing and its becoming as an other. 68] Lenz is walking on his head, the sky beneath him as abyss; severed heads are tossed into a basket, an inavowable community to come. 69] Danton, Camille, the others—they all have words, many artful words; they make them stick, in confirmation of both "puppet" and "string."

70] To hold forth in unartful words: "The presencing of a person as language, realization of language as person" in "the opacity of what is at hand."

## VIII

71] Now we are working in isolation, in a room with others who are doing the same; we pause to listen to one of us; now we are dying in isolation. 72] In *The Dark*, a German science fiction thriller TV series dating from the 2010s, a nuclear power plant has shut down, opening a fissure in the historical present that allows us to leap decades, back to a former time. 73] In a totally different era, the same art appears yet again on the stage, presented by a carnival barker, but taking the shape of a monkey, which we immediately recognize by its coat and trousers, and you are like him. 74] The poem: a language fragment that has become mortal, beyond art, starting a route into nothingness, allowing a gap to arise that gives form to the new, to what follows, as art. 75] What stops everything, what gets in the way, is the Medusa's head of all imitation, which one wishes one were: "to grasp the natural as natural" with the help of representation. 76] The poem's hour of birth, *meine Damen und Herren*, lies in darkness—not the darkness just before dawn, but darkness of itself, as it is. 77] Just as Lucile, who is blind to all artfuless, but whose language has something personal and tangible, speaks on the rostrum of her scaffold the contrary word, a word cut off from its "string," that no longer bows down to "the bystanders and war-horses of history": her "Vive le roi!" affirms herself. 78] "Die Mauern stehn / Sprachlos und kalt": an ending as true today as it was in former times; it could represent the coming ages equally well. 79] The meridian is the historicity of an event that persists by means of the destruction of the date, both "the acute of today, the grave of history." 80] The poem fills itself with the darkness of what stands opposite, the wall: it is an immobile language-block, facing us as silent catastrophe.

## IX

81] The poem offers itself up to an interlinear version, reading the space between lines; he begs you to understand these empty lines between verse and verse as *spatial* and *temporal*—a serial unfolding. 82] In another time, I would stop for a while in *Buchhandlung Gastl*, where collected works line the walls and Celan debates with Benjamin, Bloch, Arendt, and Adorno. 83] Then one evening in the tower overlooking the Neckar where Hölderlin went mad, I gave my reading of *Atemwende* as a parallel to the cries of a howler monkey, experienced on a recent trip to Costa Rica. 84] The poem will be a sending forth of oneself toward oneself, in search of oneself, up to and including the time of its understanding, uniting all interpretation in the event. 85] *Als ob er fragt*, "Does one take, when thinking of poems, does one take such routes with the poems?" *dann die Antwort war*: "They are encounters, routes of a voice to a perceiving you, creaturely routes, blueprints for being perhaps." 86] In these regions of meaning, or sites of a question being asked, his defense of a poetics "like a higher Esperanto," a *Funkdichtung* of ultralanguage is set against the hawked, dissyllabled, modernity of speech. 87] Sound and meaning, sense and interpretation, collapse on the meridian; just so rhythmic processes may be released but can never be predetermined. 88] What can be reached through language enters into an indissociable bond with a person's speechlessness, voiced and voiceless at the same time, the wish to gain the world and the wish, the ur-original wish of the poet, thus the poem, to be free of it. 89] "The card which is the / four of hearts must / mean enduring experience / of life. What other / meaning could it have," wrote Robert Creeley in *Pieces*, framing the fullness of the lyric against the unspoken "half of life," after Hölderlin. 90] Everywhere what cannot be spoken is energetic and alive, working its way through the archive into the dark light of the poem, radioactive.

## X

91] "The Meridian" in its archive—"Das Land in den See"—emerges as a firmament out of the fluid body of the *heteronomous* to be embellished of "free beauties"—"ihr holden Schwäne." 92] The revolutionary suicide of *Danton's*

*Death* is rescripted as a Cold War allegory of Mutually Assured Destruction, splitting East from West over an existential faultline. 93] In the posthumous writings Celan's poetics continue to signify, arriving at an inorganic state of matter, "the realm of the most essential turning-toward the one speaking in the poem." 94] The person speaking in the poem is not an object or a substantial kind of being but only *in* and *through* his acts, a continuously self-executing unfolding structure. 95] I climbed the cobbled streets overlooking the town to the student café, only to be perplexed by a red-and-black image of Adorno presiding over an evening of speed-dating. 96] Breathlessly, and by the greed that they are alive, he became a legend in his time, "voiceful—voiceless" simultaneously, disappearing at the very moment his message was received, prefigured in every hybridity, "finite—infinite." 97] *Unendlichsprechend* is the condition of the poet, absent any boundaries, his serial transgressions concealed within an opaque language that continues without let or cease. 98] "The poem is literally that which *speaks-itself-to-death*": what consolation is there for taking this impossible route, leading ever outward, risking sense and consequence? 99] "Und wo // Den Sonnenschein, / Und Schatten der Erde?": the region of the poem annexes being but is never reducible to it, a supplement of the only order it can permit. 100] The question of poetics "stays open," "does not come to an end," "points toward the open, empty, free": that poem alone finds a place in the archive, for I am talking about a poem that does not exist!

*in memory of Pierre Joris*

# Unthought

What was the use? Terrifying thoughts assailed me, thoughts which were taking a definite shape. I no longer told myself, "It's a dream." I had ceased to believe that. Now I was thinking: "I must be ready to defend myself."

—Stanislaw Lem, *Solaris*

## I

*What was the use?* The imperative to "darken it,"
    whatever data of consciousness concerns . . .
Attack givens thus. They are always undermined
    by what comes next, as earlier a fantasy . . .
Counted objections. A noble predator in academic
    garb who has truly misused his power . . .
Brings them together. Inviting many young women
    to their lifelong doom, permanent doubt . . .
Imposter syndrome. And such was this specimen,
    caught up in a tissue of lies and projection . . .
Equipped with sensors. Her need for his defense,
    a hollow pit surrounded by specters . . .
Of emotional distress. Being manipulated beyond
    her will, she was powerless to ward off . . .
But in harm's way. Far beyond the limits of her
    knowledge, a door or barrier between . . .
May strike targets. These specters were herself,
    or versions of herself not of his doing . . .
An ethical standard. A disturbance that continues
    to throw up new shapes, dissolving at will . . .

## II

*Terrifying thoughts*. Each more terrifying than the
next, a daisy chain or extended sequence . . .
Punctuating agency. To what source in the text
should we appeal and how to arrange it . . .
Identifying desire. Let us put our finger on what
went wrong so that we may correct it . . .
Being as humans. A voice in the mirror makes sense
in reverse if only to disappear at once . . .
Material objects. We are caught up in perspectives
that insufficiently address our liminal state . . .
Not a binary. As easily as the surface of a mirror
can be displaced by mere tilting it away . . .
Uneven agency. Each one takes away something
from themselves, a theory of knowledge . . .
But not cognition. While she pours out words of
complaint without let or hindrance . . .
Bodies enmeshed. While he pours out words of
compliance, a door slams shut on him . . .
Anonymous flux. Forms of life that insufficiently
address their illusion of being there . . .

## III

*Assailed me, thoughts.* Let us say what we think we
mean to address as always incomplete . . .
Have not changed. The phenomena that disturb us,
since the day I had seen her the last time . . .
Even in a dream. Have I done the necessary work
to expose their arguments and counter-logics . . .
We evolve into. I could not bring myself to touch a
living person who rendered herself to me . . .
Predictable error. What is the hell I am in if only
other people not contradictory to me . . .
Emptied of meaning. The text cycles through its
positions in a frame constructing display . . .
Uneven activity. Each layer operates dynamically
to influence others in all places at all times . . .
Expressing itself. The only question is whether to
remain suspended or descend forthwith . . .
Technical questions. I was dreaming, I was aware
that I was dreaming, but even in a dream . . .
Which persists. I would have preferred that she not
be there, I closed my eyes not to seem . . .

## IV

*Taking definite shape*. There was a scandal in the
academy and all the members knew of it . . .
Decision trees. "I have a feeling I have forgotten
something; I've forgotten lots of things" . . .
Nested inside. This is a situation I must address,
within the academic community . . .
"If" that is true. Reduced to a series of stylized
expressions, gestures, and movements . . .
Unlike "else." Walking into the room where they
hold their meetings, I was unaware of it . . .
Cycles nonstop. Part of a single whole, everything
he had experienced, discovered, or guessed . . .
24/7/365. He had been removed from the academy
and all his friends were aware of it . . .
Automatic reply. "I have the feeling something's
happened; I can only remember a sum" . . .
Metastable states. That had been prefigured for him
many times, completely and conclusively . . .
Thinking within. To discover the solution to this
problem means to exit from it for all time . . .

## V

*I no longer believe.* We are the cause of our own
    suffering, an amplifier of our dreams . . .
A cognitive process. "She refused to make scenes."
    In the middle of night, suddenly awake . . .
Information repeats. This is true of all unknowns;
    they cannot represent themselves . . .
Interpreting pain. Her face screwed up in agony,
    she loses consciousness again. She faints . . .
Redundant signals. 7 A.M.: "I had no idea how long
    I had been lying there awake in the dark" . . .
Zeroes and ones. The mind depends on preconscious
    sensors, traces of movement and repose . . .
Require context. "I am not staring with eyes wide
    open at a bare light on a blank screen" . . .
Meaning is made. Multiple pain sensors on and off,
    a sliding scale or rheostat of sense data . . .
As constructed. Nerves are analogs until they tip
    the scale from its off to on position . . .
In thin air. I am only half thinking this, he thinks.
    Questioning nature, we learn from it . . .

## VI

*As in a dream.* An empty grey arena ringed by a
crowd of onlookers on tiers of seats . . .
As an example. Space is an extent of imagination,
a mode of learning distributed over time . . .
In a series. I am following a long empty corridor,
not intending to glorify human choice . . .
To give an order. Because there may be thoughts,
intentions and cruel hopes in my mind . . .
Mix with water. Of which I can know nothing,
because I am a murderer unawares . . .
To make cement. It is his pleasure to write what he
thinks, to be thinking along with it . . .
Force of a pulley. It is her dilemma to speak of a
condition she can know nothing about . . .
As the rope. "A name, unfamiliar to me, had been
underlined in red: André Berton" . . .
Striking a flame. Our names are only ghosts of
ourselves, of our acts, our past histories . . .
Breaking down. A new discovery can but follow
from our discontinuous prompts . . .

## VII

*To have ceased.* Knowledge held in common by all
members of the team, thinking as one . . .
In many voices. A large red spot appears on the
dying sun, an event we cannot foretell . . .
As a prompt. With a single command, an operator
can change a whole network of signals . . .
Changed to same. While he would never listen to
her podcast, recorded for all posterity . . .
Smoothly flows. The dwarf magnolia is in bloom,
about the same time it bloomed last year . . .
Traffic deaths. Young person on motorcycle rides
past the window, into the wind, uphill . . .
Not possible. This is the present you decided it
would be, from a long time in the past . . .
*Raison d'être.* A conversation grows in his mind as
any likelihood of her reply grows less . . .
Poison cures. This is our situation *vis à vis* nature:
it is not "like" us, cannot answer back . . .
Value to values. The mind of the mnemonist, in
comparison with the instincts of a dog . . .

## VIII

*It is not thought.* What an animal already knows,
  and that you are not required to tell it . . .
If we decide. Without exploring his own labyrinth
  of dark passages and secret chambers . . .
When it is time. Without finding what lies behind
  doorways which he himself has sealed . . .
Requires a link. Over bare fields of an unforgiving
  land, explosions may erupt in any place . . .
Or disconnect. Patience and fortitude, dear God, as
  I am stranded on this mountain you made . . .
Erase machine. After their man-made catastrophe,
  a turn to such explanations is marked . . .
Assassin suicides. Face turned upward, beseeching
  the sky, this is the face of realism today . . .
*L'amour fou.* The destiny of woman is choice; all
  human history descends from that fact . . .
Catachresis. An *eidolon* of desire both ways, stands
  for all human needs at the same time . . .
Similar scale. The woman's choice, in the event, was
  to disappear from the face of the earth . . .

## IX

*I am prepared.* He cannot unthink these thoughts,
as they are attacking him from all sides . . .
On auto-pilot. "A gigantic Black woman is coming
silently after us with smoothly rolling gait" . . .
Protocols end. "It is possible for thinking to exist
without awareness of its being thought" . . .
Chance procedure. "The Whiteness of the page is
hurting me, I can only stare into the sun" . . .
Defining abyss. "That is how the dream begins. All
around me, something awaits my consent" . . .
Artificial sleep. "Is this the experiment that's on
your mind, that you continue to perform?" . . .
Somatic gaze. "The more silence seems to promise,
the more terrible the outcome will be" . . .
Intelligent machines. "Are there other worlds like
this?" "This is the only world we know" . . .
Piloting drones. "I believe too that this presence
manifests itself as powerfully in dreams" . . .
Detecting lies. I can only half think these thoughts,
so I have decided to write them down . . .

## X

*To defend myself.* My doctoral thesis received a fair
amount of attention, not all of it kind . . .
The dark ocean. Out of the mass of general mental
processes, he distilled despair, pleasure, fear . . .
Its primal mist. "The sum total of known facts was
strictly negative," as we read in the text . . .
Tremors spread. I wanted to show how negativity
and progress intertwine in the modern age . . .
Strange waves rise up. "Love," she said, "what's
happening to us? No half-truths, promise!" . . .
In blue-green foam. When it arrives, the visitor is
almost blank, a ghost made up of its sources . . .
Membranous wings. "I know enough to realize I am
not a human being, only an instrument" . . .
Or silken scarf. My name is coupled with grotesque
headlines mocking ideas I once had had . . .
As if ocean itself were mutating. Their connection
was epiphenomenal, nothing more nor less . . .
Or shedding a skin. "So that you won't forget that I
am the one who is here; I am not her" . . .

*in memory of Cole Heinowitz*

# Orphée in Translation

I

You're being stupid—
Stop asking questions.
Ne posez pas de questions
In the Café des poètes.

II

The dumb motorcyclists.
Mais tu dors certainment.
Do they know who I am?
Answer: je suis ta mort.

III

Five raps in quick succession.
Counting 38, 39, 40: I repeat.
Orphée rejects pure numbers.
Il n'y a pas d'autre station.

IV

C'est Orphée et Heurtebise
En ruine, les mains tendues.
Where are we? Our life is one
Long death. This is the zone.

## V

About one hour in come the
Fatal words—les mots justes.
What do you mean by "poet"?
To write not being a writer.

## VI

Overvoice intones: the zone
Is a concrete no-man's-land.
The descent into the zone is a
Tour-de-force mise-en-scène.

## VII

Greetings! You're smashed!
You're brave to speak to me.
I have nothing new to say.
En fait, ils me détestent.

## VIII

Stage direction: an order
To an actor playing a part.
The actor speaks his part—
Ce qui se passe se déroule.

## IX

No legend is entitled to be
Beyond its time and place—
Interpret it any time later.
Entrent Heurtebise et Cegeste.

## X

He's twenty-two years old
And admired by all. La mort,
La Princesse veut emmener
Sa classe de jeunes hommes.

## XI

As long as we ask questions
We remain alive! —En route!
Not-poems will be the place
For our unasked questions.

## XII

He looks badly wounded.
I advise you to disappear!
Ne fais pas de remarques.
The hospital is behind us.

## XIII

A composite multi-frame
Concoted of optical games
Where cinematic space is
Fluide, réversible, subjectif.

## XIV

It is made of men's memories
Les ruines de leurs habitudes.
Every mirror in the world leads
Here, one can only suppose.

## XV

A dead man in the next room
And the men who killed him.
Le parti pris de chose qui veut
Tearing him limb from limb.

## XVI

Elle m'a dit qu'elle déteste
La poésie, ne me laissant rien.
I have every right to ask for
An explanation, as do you.

## XVII

Un seul verre d'eau illumine
Le monde. Drink this water
To illuminate the world and
I repeat: un seul verre d'eau.

## XVIII

Cegeste, get up. From now on
You will be an automatic man
An automaton; tu me serviras.
Yes, I will obey your orders.

## XIX

Les motards stupides boivent
Une seule pression à Detroit.
Their beliefs are automatic
Guests of the Thermal Hotel.

## XX

The ruination and abyss of
All knowledge turning into
Force-fields and frequencies
Derrière lui, il doit traverser.

## XXI

We are his thoughts, mourir.
In our world no one is moved.
An empty table of judges, only
To turn from judge to judge.

## XXII

Dans la mythologie antique,
Orphée est un poète de Thrace.
Jean Marais holds up a mirror
To Bill Berkson, looking back.

## XXIII

Who can say what a poet is?
Quelque chose que je regrette.
The phone rings, it's Cegeste
Reading his numbers asleep.

## XXIV

Are you in love with an idea?
Sont-ils amoureux d'une idée?
"La Belle Dame sans merci"—
Title of a ballad by Keats.

## XXV

Your phrases are exquisite—
But where are your gloves?
Existant sur une page séparée
In the manual of surrealism.

## XXVI

On imagine que c'est le centre
De l'univers—of course it is.
Fulfillment in order and strife
As a matter for police action.

## XXVII

Ici seulement on ne ment pas.
All questions will be answered.
An involuntary memory is the
Lineament of gratified desire.

## XXVIII

Eurydice is only a mention
In the poem where she is lost.
A reporter from *The Daily Sun*
Passe à côté d'un tournesol.

## XXIX

I should have stayed dead!
Je suis déjà mort! I cannot be
Revived, it is all over for me.
We can't be in the same room!

## XXX

I can't be in the same world!
Tout est différent chez nous.
To read a book in the dark—
To undergo a short blackout.

## XXXI

The poet's first lines look back
Vers lui: the orange light on
The blue coast. Le dernier vers
Qu'il lit: sea blizzard at night.

## XXXII

Cegeste's last lines. In his car
Some messages are received.
They are tearing him apart.
Ça devait arriver—language.

## XXXIII

Not to mention the Princess
Who keeps us in thrall. Vous—
Merci de vous rendre inutile.
Go start a literary movement.

## XXXIV

Call the manager for me! We
Want to speak to the manager!
My husband can't be disturbed
Qu'il a travaillé toute la nuit.

## XXXV

I have been sent by *The Sun*.
Words are a perfect marriage.
Your fortune will be to travel
Une longue file de voitures.

## XXXVI

100, 101, 102. Jupiter rage—
Spilling tears over the carpet
Until the clock breaks apart.
Wallpaper hiding its secret.

## XXXVII

Orphée, si vous l'abandonnez
C'est normal qu'elle appelle
All those who love her. But
Who am I to advise you that?

## XXXVIII

Comme écrit, I am he whose
Brains scattered everywhere.
To record an involuntary line.
Un homme blessé qui dort.

## XXXVIX

Twice. I repeat. Seems nothing
But meaningless sounds to me.
Once. I repeat. I've forgotten—
Cadavre sur les lieux du crime.

## XL

What fascinating poetry! Qui
Peut dire ce qu'est la poésie et
N'est pas. Bring in the sirens!
We are dead and don't notice.

## XLI

The bird sings with its finger.
Death returns in the mirror.
Tu ne regardes pas en arrière.
A mirror is a key refrain here.

## XLII

L'oiseau chante avec son doigt.
La mort revient dans le miroir.
Do not look back on pain of—
Un miroir est un principe ici.

## XLIII

An idea! What do I want with—
Qu'est-ce que je veux avec une.
Irma Vep in cat burgler outfit
Predates all Paris on a rooftop.

## XLIV

In the philosophical tradition
Un poète manqué n'est pas un
Bête. The poet is the director
Of a film entirely in his head.

## XLV

I have been given no orders.
There's a little room above the
Garage, you can park your car
Et attends qu'elle se montre.

## XLVI

Je suis peut-être idiot mais
Je suis sûr de certaines choses.
Butter is bread on its other side
Of a toaster that cries for help.

## XLVII

Opening credits for Orphée.
Driving into the negative then
Driving backwards, je conduis
À reculons dans le négatif.

## XLVIII

Et en avant. She passes me by
In a convertible, slows down
Until she is in vocable range,
Giving me signs to pull over.

## XLIX

La Princesse et Heurtebise.
Un chauffeur ne donne pas
Ses propres ordres. Wake-up!
This is the car and I'm driving.

## L

Cegeste! Won't you ever learn
Not to turn back? Les gens ont
Été transformés en pilier de sel
For less. Character is destiny!

## LI

Character transforms destiny
Dans l'acte de traduction. Title
Of a literary magazine in the
High modern era: *transition*.

## LII

Jean Cocteau never appeared
In *transition* under that name
But delegated his admirers to
Write un œuvre pseudonyme.

## LIII

There is something shady and
Second hand about this affair,
Cria Orphée en route sur Terre
En chemin, to retrieve his wife.

## LIV

Mais il ne devait pas être. To
Click the button in automatic
Translate is like a photograph.
Ecstatic moment of othering.

## LV

But the guys / lay them aside
For radios. Jeune homme triste
Dans un train, thinking ahead
What comes next: sa carrière.

## LVI

The motorcyclists of destiny:
Poètes et peintres stupides.
Each one delivers themselves
To their fate, unconsciously.

## LVII

In the pattern of everyday life
To do one thing after the next.
But Aglaonise est dangereuse
Avec her League of Women.

## LVIII

Je fais juste ce qui est normal
Until I wake up in the extreme
Finality of a situation I ought
To have admitted long ago.

## LIX

The message is delivered, final.
Dites mois la verité. She wants
Me under her thumb for good
Reason. You fume like a ghost.

## LX

Sa métier: I am no chauffeur
But a student who suicided
After reading Kathy Acker
In the library of the convent.

## LXI

My lost love was a barrage of
Symbols, a demon of analogy.
Numbers are the measure of X.
Je ne trouve pas cette station.

## LXII

Le paradigme du mensonge.
You move, but are motionless.
Glazier! A man who trades in
Illusions of glass for a living.

## LXIII

Are they alive? These Nazis
But speak perfect French or
Version of same, mais leurs
Mots n’ont aucun sens ici.

## LXIV

I loved you even before we met.
I loved you infinitely, no more
No less. Inexplicable—I must
Now seem very stupid to you.

## LXV

I loved my love and our great
Undoing, you are all-powerful.
Ils disent qu'ils pensent à nous
And that we are their thoughts.

## LXVI

Dis "toujour." Je jure. Swear
On this stack of Bibles—swear
Or affirm that what you testify
In this inquiry is the truth.

## LXVII

Poubelle ce stupide email!
To look at myself in a mirror.
The denigration of vision: not
Willing to live with shades.

## LXVIII

Signs in the street say where
You're going. Heurtebise leads
Orphée where he will not go.
Ici et ailleurs, étant le leur.

## LXIX

You never mention Eurydice—
Surely she suffers too! But if
She suffers, how do I know?
Il n'y a que moi qui parle.

## LXX

From Eurydice, no messages
Sauf sa présence éternelle
That would disappear at once
As we know, as we were told.

## LXXI

Où aucun message ne vient.
This is the zone. All messages
Come from the zone, at every
Turn forced back, forced on.

## LXXII

Beaucoup de gens me trouvent
Insupportable! Pauvre petit—
They love you. Unaccountably
The stars say "Jean Cocteau."

## LXXIII

Je cherche l'or du temps, où?
My name a death's head and
The line is a crux. De quoi?
Two roads diverge in a line.

## LXXIV

Two languages diverge in a
Sentence. La phrase nouvelle.
Characters are only bundles
Of features on a book cover.

## LXXV

Orphée, Cegeste, Heurtebise,
La Princesse n'existent plus.
A curtain call at the Comédie
Française, boring centuries.

## LXXVI

I have achieved dénouement—
Now well past it. Cities in ruins.
When they arrest you, it's not
Pleasant—n'est jamais agréable.

## LXXVII

We could die and they would
Not notice. It's all in the sound.
Détails d'un vers de *The Wedge*
By the great American poet.

## LXXVIII

Jupiter donne de la sagesse
To those he would lose. I am
Not the only ridiculous one!
Don't forget the apparatus!

## LXXIX

Sir! This sentence is a poem!
Day of the accident his head
Was smashed in order to give
Directives à toute l'humanité!

## LXXX

Il y a deux types d'universaux.
The one in the other—a game
Invented by poets to confound
Materialists of the opposition.

## LXXXI

We are not there yet. Soon!
The grief of young widows is
As brief as a noonday candle.
The preeminent littérateur.

## LXXXII

Une fois, tout aurait peut être.
I demand absolute discipline—
As on a ship, you have orders.
These are not my lines, he said.

## LXXXIII

The mirror is only you! I am
Confused, as in a Bengal light.
Il n'y a rien à faire! Our love
Is like bees in a hive of glass.

## LXXXIV

A poet is more than a man—
You have only one chance left
To find her again. As in death—
Un des visages de la Princesse.

## LXXXV

In our world no one is named.
Aimez vous cette femme? I am
Not that person. You are guilty
Of love for a person, sign here.

## LXXXVI

Orphée, there is no person.
You are not a person, having
No right to personhood. Only
Lui dont les mots peuvent tuer.

## LXXXVII

I overstepped my authority.
What do you say in response?
Ce n'était que circonstanciel—
Unperson at the wrong time.

## LXXXVIII

Unperson writes a not-poem.
We are the pseudo-universals
That make our laws. Perhaps—
Il n'y a pas de "peut-être" ici.

## LXXXIX

Come forward! Je ne voulais
Pas désobéir. Your profession?
Poet. The card says "writer."
What do you mean by "poet"?

## XC

The poet is he who writes for
Anyone to know it is written.
On peut être n'importe qui—
It could even be Heurtebise.

## XCI

C'est la non-identité en soi
That speaks solely pour soi.
You are now free to go, but
On condition never to speak.

## XCII

Vous avez les gants, mettez-les.
They are merely an illustration
Signifying the burning of Paris
During the Commune of 1871.

## XCIII

The Zero Hour is rare in life—
At which we begin again. Using
Artificial means une traduction
Of zero hour any time of life.

## XCIV

Au-delà la trahison des clercs.
His compliance may be possible
To observe, under watchful eye
With continuous supervision.

## XCV

Here Eros is raised to a power
Of abstract laws and destiny.
C'est effrayant, dit Heurtebise.
It is the mirror of culpability.

## XCVI

You must be blind to the truth
And all desire, and never look
For any proof of innocence or
Guilt—car ils sont identiques.

## XCVII

The nonidentity that is to be
The nonidentity to come, as if
They are identical. Une lettre
Anonyme cachée sous la table.

## XCVIII

It is a letter for you, from one
You are forbidden to love. It is
Eurydice hiding in the garden
En flagrant délit avec Cegeste.

## XCIX

At least as one can imagine it.
According to the Princess, il ne
Faut pas parler de telles choses.
Alexandrines sleep on the sofa.

## C

La pitié et la terreur résolvent
Un conflit. Its proportions are
Precise and various, like lines
And their lives in translation.

## Some / Ruins

GROUND

Abyss.

FACT

Value.

FORCE

Matter.

EVIDENCE

Psychosexual.

REVERIE

Engineer.

ALTERTUM

Wissenschaft.

CHRISTENTUM

Paganismus.

RELATION

Ramp.

FORCE

Interrogation.

LISTENING

Hard.

BELLS

Zvuki.

PURSUED

Fury.

SEXUALITY

Correlation.

BEGRIFF

Concept.

STIMMUNG

Stimmt.

CONFERENCE

Badge.

LINEATION

Lines.

SHINOLA

Notebook.

PEDAGOGY

Failure.

SAD

Archive.

FANTASIE

Travail.

AS

If.

ALS

Ob.

LOGICAL

Particle.

NOUMENA

Schein.

BODY

Object.

BLOCKED

Text.

TRIPLE

Zed.

MOB

Justice.

DISCREDIT

Goal.

THRUST

Lift.

GAP

Fissure.

SCHWERPUNKT

Hysteria.

ÜBERMORGEN

Translation.

ZOOFACHMARKT

Petstore.

BOOK

Title.

MAO

Pacific.

OVERFLOW

Simulacrum.

SHUN

Actant.

DDR

Curtains.

PROFESSOR

Under.

HEADLINE

News.

AND

Exposed.

SIEGE

Negative.

BROKEN

Melodrama.

HOUSE

Unhappiness.

TRANSFERENCE

Inference.

MY

Ocean.

OUTER

Inner.

PUERILE

Core.

FORTIFIED

Play.

RADICAL

Particular.

NEGATIVE

Plateau.

LOOKING

Glass.

LIBERAL

Adjustment.

DISPLAY

Person.

SERVICE

Self.

SILO

Engorgement.

HUMAN

Type.

INUIT

Eskimo.

TIMELINE

Event.

ENTIÈREMENT

Volllustig.

JUST

Compensation.

SHADOW

Law.

BELATED

Charisma.

ACCEPT

Cookies.

SHAPE

Shifter.

ALIGN

Alone.

TIBER

Cloaca.

FURNITURE

Stacked.

RETHINK

Example.

UNREMOVABLE

Malware.

TRICKSTER

Gaslight.

QUARANTINE

Knots.

DEATH

Series.

PARTICULARS

Cling.

OPEN

Monument.

SUBTEXT

Alarm.

DECISION

Nihil.

CRUX

Rock.

SUBJECT

Predicate.

REVERSE

Opposite.

ACÉPHALE

Psychoactive.

SENS

Plastique.

CODDLE

Preciosity.

MAKER

Lament.

COMPLIANT

Complaint.

FEROCIOUS

Dogma.

BASSIN

Villette.

RESTAURANT

Fabricants.

FOLIE

Jour.

MAIRIE

Mensonge.

CONVERSATION

Dream.

LOST

Decade.

FICHE

Moi.

CANCEL

This.

DIALECTIC

Reason.

PROJECT

Site.

BEVÖLKERUNG

Volk.

GOVERNMENT

Whole.

HUSBAND

Boyscout.

SPECIES

Genre.

GENRE

Species.

GITLER

Durak.

PARENT

Child.

NOT

Child.

NOT

Parent.

CHILD

Parent.

TRIFECTA

Lies.

VOID

Coefficient.

HORROR

Vacui.

DISSOLVE

Speak.

STATE

Mistake.

NEGRITUDE

Victoria.

IT

Wittgenstein.

INNUENDO

Calculus.

ADORNO

Lacan.

SEMINAR

Facebook.

CLIENT

Base.

SERVICE

Provision.

QUESTION

Answer.

DEMAND

Lack.

THOUSAND

Billion.

LIGHT

Dark.

EDUCATE

Words.

MEMORY

Amnesia.

SOME

Ruins.

LIKE

Language.

*homage to Robert Grenier*

# Notes / Sources / Publications / Credits

## [I]
Period Style

NOTES: "Period Style" originated as a composite work, a *correlation* as I use the term, between two early texts. The first is "Furniture Cards," a set of 3½ x 5½" index cards on which I pasted cut-out furniture advertisements with rubber cement. The date is c. 1973, on my arrival in San Francisco, a testament to bare nothing at the beginning date of this collection. I correlated these image cards with framed samples from a series of three one-paragraph prose poems written later that decade: "After the Fact," "New Apartments," and "The Cure," published in *Roof* 5, ed. James Sherry (1978). As there has been some discoloring due to oxidation of both paper and cement in the originals, the images are not reproduced here.

The title itself responds to Charles Altieri and other critics who used the term *period style* for Language writing as part of its contested reception. I responded in *Questions of Poetics*, where the term appears numerous time in the index, and later online:

> Even at the origins of Language writing, we must reject the notion that its contributions were merely a *period style*; numerous modernist and postmodern authors undertook writing projects that foreground language in similar ways. An origin is a historical, cultural, and aesthetic complex that can never be adequately recovered, but only retrospectively constructed—in the process of which, the difference between Language writing as an active method and the static description of a *period style* comes clear.

I go on to locate and quote each instance where the term occurs in *Questions of Poetics*, concluding: "The opposite principle, which I use to read Language writing and many other art practices, from Allen Ginsberg's journals to On Kawara's date paintings to Tracie Morris's sound poetry, John Cage's *Etudes australes*, and Wolf Eyes' noise music, is *critical art practice*. A 'critical art practice' is one that reflexively examines its basic assumptions of language, form, genre, medium, identity, culture, history, and so on." A good test would be the stylistic device of the "New Sentence," which was first understood as a critical art practice.

SOURCES: advertising supplement, *San Francisco Chronicle*, c. 1973; notebooks; *Questions of Poetics: Language Writing and Consequences* (U Iowa P, 2016); "Document 73: Period Style," *barrettwatten.net*, 18 June 2018, http://bit.ly/2HW6KJq.

Publications: "After the Fact," "New Apartments," "The Cure," *Roof* (ed. James Sherry) 5 (1978).

## [II]
## War of Position

Notes: "War of Position" dates my first use of *correlation*, for a work based on the juxtaposition of two texts and the new meaning that results, from 1981. I do not recall the specific impulse that led me to use individual sentences from my poem "Position" to sample, and then interpret, complete paragraphs from Tolstoy's *War and Peace*. I was interested, however, in expanding the "unit structure" of the New Sentence as theorized by Ron Silliman, and demonstrated in 1970s Language writing by Carla Harryman, Lyn Hejinian, Silliman, me, and others. I wanted to see how the shifted form of the New Sentence of my 144-line poem "Position"—composed of 96 sentences broken into irregular phrases by the modular stanza form, as reduced to metalanguage as possible—could unpack the narrative frames of Tolstoy's paragraphs and interpret them in some way. Viktor Shklovsky's *Theory of Prose*, from which Hejinian and I published an excerpt in the first issue of *Poetics Journal*, but also his biography *Lev Tolstoy* (1978, Progress Publishers), which I found at a Russian-language bookstore in San Francisco, were also motivations. I also do not recall how I sampled the text, likely using a table of random numbers from a chemistry handbook I had from college, but the first results showed a deep correspondence. I followed the lead of the pairings in sequence and worked my way through the poem and novel. Reading the work decades later, I see it now as not only a linguistic but cultural critique: the structuralist politics of "language" against the nineteenth-century realist novel and its political, class, and gender assumptions. The poet, after Marx's Theses on Feuerbach, seeks to interpret the world as a precondition for changing it.

Sources: Leo Tolstoy, *War and Peace*, trans. Louise and Aylmer Maude (1923; Norton, 1966); "Position," in *1–10* (This, 1980).

Publications and readings: "Position," *This* 10 (1980); *1–10*; excerpt trans. Jean-Pierre Faye, *Change* (Paris) 41 (March 1981); *In the American Tree*, ed. Ron Silliman (National Poetry Foundation, 1986); excerpt trans. Faye, in *MAM.R.C. Bulletin littérature* (Paris; ed. Emmanuel Hocquard) 201 (1989); *Onward: Contemporary Poetry and Poetics*, ed. Peter Baker (Peter Lang, 1996); *Frame (1971–1990)* (Sun & Moon, 1997); "Correlation of 'Position' and *War and Peace*," hand-made book, Xerox with cover and end sheets, stapled, dated 7–18 July 1981; read at Small Press Traffic, San Francisco, 1981; parts 1–15, in *Barrett Watten: Contemporary Poetics as Critical Theory*, *Aerial* (ed. Rod Smith) 8 (1995).

## [III]

### Question of Interpretation

Notes: This poem records the visionary state (or oceanic feeling) that followed my one week's residency at the Naropa Summer Writing Program, June 2003. I wrote multiple individual stanzas in a notebook and then transferred them to index cards, then culled and arranged the stanzas. A bit later, Detroit artist Deb King asked me for work for her online journal *Mark(s)*. I proposed pairing the stanzas of the poem with miniature inkblots I had made about age 8, which I had recently rediscovered; they are my personal Rorschach test. For the web site, which is no longer active, King devised a display where the inkblot images when clicked on would rotate and disappear into nothing, then reappear: a visualization of the *fort/da* itself. Correlative to this visualization, I recall my public reading at Naropa, which I introduced by holding, in a proper and respectful manner as confirmed by my hosts, a small Tibetan *dorje* ("diamond thunderbolt") which I was inspired to use by my tutelary spirit in Vajrayana Buddhism (and found at a local Tibet shop in Boulder). The poem is dedicated to the memory of my cousin Martin, who died while performing a three-year *puja* in the Tibetan Buddhist retreat at Dordogne, France—where I visited him in 1978. Martin also spoke at my mother's funeral in 1990, where he pronounced, with careful framing for non-Buddhists, a one-word mantra in Tibetan as a blessing. The poem's concern with nonexistence owes everything to my cousin's influence and example. For publication here, I decided not to include the twelve inkblots as interpretants, as their color combinations would not display well in black and white.

Sources: inkblot cards; notebooks.

Publications and readings: "Question of Interpretation" (interactive poem), *Mark(s)* (ed. Deb King) 4, no. 4 (2004); link inactive; "Questions d'interprétation," trans. Martin Richet, read at Double Change, Paris, 2009.

## [IV]

### Blue States (After Fearing)

Notes: I wrote "Blue States" as a correlation between Popular Front poet Kenneth Fearing and the results of 2004 election, which confirmed George W. Bush for a second term. Fearing, along with Muriel Rukeyser, is a central figure in the recovery of the poetry of the Left in the 1930s, after literary historians such as Cary Nelson and Walter Kalaidjian. I featured Fearing's work in my teaching at Wayne State University and experienced a strong response from working-class students who got his pathos and criticality; I also showed *The Big Clock* in a number of classes. Fearing had a problematic biography: unstable but broadly public; subject to highs and lows that he interpreted as Depression-era politics; called before the House Un-American Activities Committee in 1950; a heavy smoker and drinker who died at age 58. "He held few full-time jobs for more than a few months, despite claiming, apparently falsely, to have worked as a salesman, a journalist, and even a lumberjack in press materials" (*Wikipedia*, s.v. "Fearing"). Fearing's 1930s melancholia was a perfect correlative to the "Blue States" we were in, emotionally but also politically, after the election. In making the work for my online website, I sampled two to four lines of Fearing's poetry and then wrote a three-line entry that reinterpreted it. In 2005, I was awarded a Fulbright to Germany, where I sought parallels in the German 1930s to the rightward turn of the Bush II Era. Fortunately Bush squandered his political capital in attempting to privatize Social Security, but the moment was a predictor of things to come. The poem is dedicated to Bill Berkson, not a Leftist, to whom I made the remark, after the election, that we ought to "paint the town blue."

†Sources: from Kenneth Fearing, *Selected Poems*, ed. Robert Polito (Library of America, 2004), printed in Gill Sans Regular: from "Dance of the Mirrors," p. 87; "A la Carte," p. 102; "The Doctor Will See You Now," p. 99; "Escape," p. 55; "The Drinkers," p. 13; "A Pattern," p. 78; "Invitation," p. 27; "Dividends," p. 39; "4 a.m.," p. 145; "Manhattan," p. 89; "Dirge," p. 51; "How Do I Feel?," p, 92; "American Rhapsody (1)," p. 37; "Lullaby," p. 58; "Sherlock Spends a Day in the Country," p. 152; "Angel Arms," p. 29; "The Program," p. 79; "Take a Letter," p. 84; "$2.50," p. 56; "Pact," p. 98; "Piano Tuner," p. 131; "C Stands for Civilization," p. 83; "Gentleman Holding Hands with Girl," p. 100; "Family Album (2)," p. 165; "Class Reunion," p. 106; "Literary," pp. 71–72; "Portrait," p. 82; "Discussion After the Fifth or Sixth," p. 113; "Portrait of a Cog," p. 101; "American Rhapsody (4)," p. 103; "Agent No. 174 Resigns," p. 97; "Public Life," p. 137; "Elegy in a Theatrical Warehouse," p. 130; "Mrs. Fanchier at the Movies," p. 154; "Radio Blues," p. 86; "Devil's Dream," p. 73; "Denouement," p. 64; "Scheherazade," p. 91; "The Juke-Box Spoke and the Juke-Box Said:," p. 148; "Ballad of the Salvation Army," p. 20; "Bryce & Tomlins," p. 151; "Readings, Forecast, Personal Guidance," p. 116; "Thirteen O'Clock," p. 122; "American Rhapsody (2)," p. 46; "Resurrection," p. 34; "Family Album (4)," p. 167; "Cracked Record Blues," p. 120; "Model for a Biography," p. 132; "Payday in the Morgue," p. 109; and "Aphrodite Metropolis," p. 11. Reprinted by the permission of Russell & Volkening as agents for the Estate of Kenneth Fearing. Copyright © 1994 by Jubal Fearing and Phoebe Fearing.

Publication: "Post 7: Blue States: Reading the Election with Kenneth Fearing," *1-Year Plan* (5 November 2004), link inactive; in special section, "Blue Year 2017: Poems," *Lana Turner* (ed. David Lau and Calvin Bedient) 10 (2018); print and online.

## [V]
## Zone (Correlation)

Notes: "In this *correlation*, I unlink by means of random numbers the continuous argument of William Carlos Williams's *Paterson*, book 1, in order to access and reconstruct its underlying (or overarching) assumptions in the present. Random numbers give me, as well, guidelines for how many lines to write in response to the samples in a form of continuous reinterpretation. The citations from *Paterson* are not 'part of the work' but links to the published text; the work may be read with or without them."

I used the above note, in several versions, as a frame text for early publications of the first part of *Zone*—a project imagined, at the outset, as a "writing through" of samples from the four core books that make up *Paterson* before its turn to "open form" in book 5. As imagined, the project is a critique of modernity through that seminal work of modernism, but it attempts more than that. In *Zone*, I wanted to map the present manifestation of modernity in Detroit as later instance of the "Society for Useful Manufactures" Alexander Hamilton imagined for Paterson. But *Zone*—neither *pater* nor *son*—is also the site of a desiring production and reproduction of information, which Williams figured in the Falls as the "throughput" of language amidst the voicelessness of democracy. As imagined, *Zone* is a project of translational modernity—from its mid-century, classic, industrial version to the postmillennial, digital, infrastructural present, as *source* to unfolding *target*. It could only be an incomplete project, so I decided to include only part 1 here, while conceptually imagining and building, in centrifugal and centripetal manner after my great forebear, around it. As may be seen, Williams is the tutelary spirit of these pages, most especially the poet of mid-career and mid-century. It is not the early Williams of formal experiment, nor the later poet of real-time presentness, but the conflicted center, from difficult verse to lucid prose, that I hold as my example.

In my imagination of *Zone*, the work is still incomplete. I have written toward its completion on many occasions, both time-based and site-specific, while its route from *source* to *target* is still being mapped. In an essay for *Grand Piano* 9, I wrote on this continuous horizon shift or crisis of ending while spacing my prose with sections of *Zone* part 2, which only there finds its way into print. The project, it seems, intends that the horizon remain open—

> For ten years I have... thought about, assembled readings for, taken notes on, and plotted structures of a long poem that is now in initial stages of composition. Its writing, though partly deferred, is a parallel track to what I am undertaking here. The genealogy of the poem—its descent from an absent origin, my intention to write it, its place in the sequence of my works—will have been an account of its materials and false starts as its emerging form. The thought of the poem begins to be the poem itself. It is the "zone" it will become—an instance of the mode of production in its spatial articulation, not the fantasy of continuous productivity that attends the individual career....
>
> To construct the initial core of *Zone*, I followed a set of sampling procedures based on his epic poem *Paterson* as a zone of poetry in mid-century modernism that reimagines modern life. Subdividing each book into sixty individual samples, I used chance procedures to randomly access them and rewrite their particularity at a level of argument I would infer in the poem's total form. The myriad particulars that we know Williams so prized and insisted on—"Say it! No ideas but in things"—are thus rewritten from the status of "pure products" to another level of argument: the metalevel of production. [T]he poem will be refunctioned in a zone I cannot entirely predict, whose additional materials and strategies have yet to be identified or disclosed. It is "in production," as I am.

"I seek not the gold of time, but the currency of history." This was how I forecast *Zone* in 2009, toward the end of *The Grand Piano*. By 2011, another horizon was manifest, the moment of radical democracy witnessed in the Occupy movement—which would coincide with the conclusion of our collective memoir. For publication in the little magazine *Armed Cell*, I described my project in presentist terms:

> In November 2011... I gave a quickly arranged house reading for Oakland poet Brian Ang, attended by some two dozen people wedged into several rooms of his apartment.... The presentation was more than inflected by the spirit of the Occupy movement and UC protests; it sought to make a direct connection, through the medium of poetics....
>
> *Zone* is a work premised on mediation, through aleatorical and improvisatory processes, of one complex political moment to another. In rereading the source text, *Paterson*, I saw Williams engaged in a meditation on the relation of poetics to democracy that may be read as much as a matter of form as con-

> tent—in terms of the shifting between poetic and documentary registers that guide the poem's inquiry. . . .
>
> In what way could the compositional processes of *Zone* (or any such processes of unlinking and recoding) intersect with the decision structures of Occupy—which constitutes its poetics, its mode of making the political (and not merely rhetoric, its mode of convincing, say, of democratic/transformative intentions)?
>
> Democracy is radicalized in Occupy in a way that has made a permanent contribution to the horizon of agency in the present—moving beyond party formations and new social movements toward a decentering of agency. . . . Radical democracy is mediation at its core, and *Zone* wants to enact its poetics through processes of transcoding one political moment to the next.

*Zone* thus aligns with radical democracy as much as translational modernism. And there are other approximations to a method that was in itself being worked out. Alongside the virtual Falls, the throughput of desire and informatics, the roar increases. I imagine this writing, this correlation, to be incomplete, but not inconclusive, as it may be.

‡Sources: Williams Carlos Williams, *Paterson* (New Directions, 1963); excerpts copyright © 1958 by William Carlos Williams; used by permission of New Directions Publishing Corp.

Publications and readings: "Post 16: Correlation of Paterson, Book 1 [excerpt]," *1-Year Plan*, 10 July 2005; link inactive; from "Correlation of *Paterson*, book 1," *Antennae* (Karlsruhe, Germ.; ed. Jesse Seldess) 9 (November 2007); from "Zone," *Edna: A Journal of Art in Residence* (Millay Colony) no. 3. (2011); from "Zone" and "Note to Zone," *Armed Cell* (ed. Brian Ang) 6 (2013); from "Zone," *The Canary Islands Connection: 60 Contemporary American Poets*, ed. Mañuel Brito (Zasterle Press, 2016); "Zona" (Zone), part 1, trans. Anna Glazova and Aleksandr Skidan, presented at Arkadii Dragomoshchenko Prize reading, St. Petersburg, November 2016; "Iz 'Zonii'" (from "Zone"), trans. Skidan, *Ot "chiornoi gori" do "yazikovo pisma": Antologiya noveishei poezii CShA* (From "Black Mountain" to "Language Writing": Anthology of New Poetry from the USA), ed. Vladimir Feshchenko and Ian Probstein (Novoe literaturnoye obozrenie [NLO], 2022); in *Not This: Selected Writings/Не то: Избранные тексты*, ed. Feshchenko (Polyphem, 2024).

## [VI]
## The Annotated "Plan B"

NOTES: From the poem's original publication in *Lana Turner*: "'Plan B' is written in an economy of 100+1 stanzas, with the keywords *Plan B, Gleichschaltung*, and *normal* or *normalize* appearing every ten stanzas. The triadic line, of course, comes from Williams, who first learned it from Mayakovsky; it was not unknown to O'Hara. Numbers are a synecdoche for poetry. *Gleichschaltung* as a concept emerged in March/April 1933 in Germany, combining psychological and institutional processes through which political subjectivity 'switched over' and was 'coordinated' in the fascist state. It influenced Adorno's notion of 'identity thinking' as a combination of reason and terror. The 'normalization' of unreason as a form of political subjectivity was what I feared would happen after November 2016.... There are also two mentions of the *Edmund Fitzgerald*, a marine disaster in the fateful year 1975, well known to the people of Michigan as an allegory of the state, and to those familiar with Gordon Lightfoot's ballad. The extent to which unreason is a necessary element of political discourse is still an open question. The precise meaning of *Plan B* is thus hermeneutical and still unfolding; we do not yet know what it will be."

"Plan B" was written in a gale of revulsion following the 2016 election, over four days in November. I felt exceptional urgency in putting forward this work, in making it as widely known as possible. I posted excerpts from the poem, and the PDF from *Lana Turner* when that was available; read it in Detroit, Chicago, Oakland, Paris, Berlin, Munich, and St. Petersburg; recorded it for a French YouTube channel; exhibited an excerpt in the form of a postcard at the Berkeley Art Museum; and worked with Franziska Ruprecht, Abigail Lang, Aleksandr Skidan, and Olga Sokolova on translations into German, French, and Russian. I wanted the poem to be a wake-up call against normalizing the election, and got into no small trouble (particularly at a rally at Wayne State University) in conveying my agitation. I would say, as well, that this agitation was widely shared, internalized as an overflowing cornucopia of fear and paranoia, which the poem imitates in its unreasonable thought and association, telegraphing from one malformed discourse to the next—a sliding of the signifier as lived reality, at a precise political and cultural moment we endured at the time. Such is the legacy of our national heritage, that it led us to such extremes. The work is pedagogical in this sense, a site for inference and argument as its underlying politics continue in new forms.

The German translation, read in Berlin and Munich, went well; Franziska Ruprecht's work as a performance artist and her knowledge of American speech idioms translated its lexical nastiness into spectacular German amalgams, which she performed in Munich. In Berlin, the poet Ulf Stolterfoht read the German, and I began to realize its departure from poetic conventions, in addition to its translational antifascism, was no small leap between literatures. For a presentation in Paris, Abigail Lang took on the rendering of its barbaric Americanisms into French, which she later confessed had tortured her to the point of cursing at the screen. We corresponded over email for weeks before the event, at which point I began to write a series of annotations to explain what may be obvious to an American but obscure in France. One such trope was the cultural divide between Red states and Blue states, which goes along with the *Gleichschaltung* thesis; if this was not obvious, what else needed to be explained? Taking a cue from the likelihood of mistranslation, I wrote a series of glosses that were, on the one hand, as excessive as the poem itself, but on the other developed a theory of its poetics. The poem was also presented at a reading in St. Petersburg in November 2016; I recall the sober expression of audience members when I explained what *Gleichschaltung* meant, in the context of the authoritarian putschism then emerging. In all cases, I wanted to encourage the poem's "effectivity" to historically intervene, as I do now.

The series of agitated performances, translations, publications came to a head at the decisive moment of January 6, 2021, the insurrection that punctuated the first four-year disaster. I noted the convergence of Rachel Maddow's use of "Plan B" in a list of options should the crisis continue, and uploaded the poem online as a further intervention. In my post, I wrote out my theory of the antidemocratic moment once again. Citing the poem's hortatory ending:

> These are the words that conclude 'Plan B,' my poem written after the 2016 election. What has transpired since could not have been more *like*—turbulence has been destiny, our demography is in pieces, and nothing is decided. It is that moment of stoppage—"the stopping / of the battle," as Charles Olson wrote—that I wanted to get down, as contribution to radical democracy perhaps. But even the concept of "radical democracy" is not now decided—that is in the nature of a decision—with the spectacle of the "mob" thinking it represents the *demos* violating "the People's House," as we have been told and can see for ourselves. My point is the instability of the moment, but also that of the discourse that represents it or attempts to intervene in it. Is that a good thing for poetry, to record such a moment, or a bad thing for politics, that its confusions may be reproduced?

Something like that occurred about the time of writing, December 2016, when I was asked to participate in a teach-in at Wayne State University ("here comes trouble" can be heard in the background, though muted). In the event, I wanted to perform a brief *intervention*—a term combining avant-garde and radical tendency—that would stop the moment and in so doing refuse to normalize the election. A politics of "refusing to normalize" had emerged at the time ("Not My President" was its slogan), which ought to have been continuously pursued, from then to now.... My second focus was the *NS* term *Gleichschaltung*, dating from March–April 1933, when both individuals and institutions "switched over" to a perversion they could scarcely comprehend, while Jews and Roma, communists and queers began to be sent to the camps. Refusing to normalize might keep *Gleichschaltung* at bay....

My presentation was informed by the state of mind I was in when I wrote the poem—channeling Adorno's *Authoritarian Personality* and trying to reverse direction by disclosing multiple strands of unreason in the discourse of the event. After an attempt to summarize Adorno's thesis—that democracy conceals and even reproduces psychological dynamics that prepare a subject to accept undemocratic politics—I tried to introduce one such psychological strain into the discourse: the famous "grab them by the [——]" remark. My point was that those voting for said person might find that shocking or unacceptable on its own terms but would vote for him nonetheless (just as said person could, as he claimed, shoot someone on Fifth Avenue and still get their vote). It was not that his constituents *believed* what he said as a positive claim; rather, it was a placeholder for *something else*—those "unfulfilled democratic demands" Laclau and Mouffe theorized, but now normalized as a form of perversion....

I had reasons for what I was trying to do; I was being *rational* in putting forth a discourse of *unreason*. In so doing I follow in the footsteps of the avant-garde, adapted to later times and modes of address. The question I raise now is the relation of the use of defamiliarization—of "not normalizing"—as a politics. I would say, given the continuing unfolding of *unreason* in public discourse that followed the 2016 election, that a mere reversal of normalization is not enough. That guy in the photo with fur hoodie, bare-chested tattoos, horns, and a six-foot-long spear is not a radical democrat—while neither was the failed intervention at the Capitol a moment of *Gleichschaltung*, though it may have been had things gone worse. At the same time, I do not agree to any form of symptomatology of the poetic attempt to "not normalize." I wrote the poem out of necessity and purpose, and it still reflects what we are subject to today.

Sources: media; automatic thinking and pure projection.

Publications and readings: "Plan B," read at Red Rover Reading Series, Chicago, November 2016; excerpt trans. Aleksandr Skidan, read at the Arkadii Dragomoshchenko Prize reading, St. Petersburg, November 2016; excerpt in "Poetics as Knowledge Base: The Example of 'Plan B,'" Louisville Conference on Literature After 1900, U Louisville (February 2017); trans. Abigail Lang, read with "Poetics as Value Thinking: Transvaluations of Language Writing," Double Change and Fondation des Etats-Unis, Paris (March 2017); trans. Franziska Ruprecht, read at JYM, Munich, July 2017, and at Lettretage, Berlin, June 2018; "Five Stanzas from PLAN B," postcard created for Way Bay exhibition, Berkeley Art Museum (January 2018); "Poetics as Value Thinking: The Example of 'Plan B.'" Humanities Center, Wayne State U (April 2018); "Plan B" with note, *Lana Turner* 12 (Fall 2018); excerpt in "The Poetics of *S P L M N T* and 'The Annotated 'Plan B,'" &Now, U Notre Dame (October 2018); from "Plan B," *Philosopher au présent* (ed. Jérôme Lèbre; 2020), YouTube video available at https://bit.ly/3fkBy8W; "Entry 43: Rolling Out Plan B," *barrettwatten.net* (10 January 2021); excerpt in "Historicism and Presentism in *Bad History* and 'The Annotated Plan B,'" École normale supérieure, Paris (November 2021); trans. Olga Sokolova, *Not This: Selected Writings/Не то: Избранные тексты*, ed. Vladimir Feshchenko (Polyphem, 2024).

## [VII]
### Media Literacy

Notes: "Media Literacy" correlates my Dada-inspired poem "Radio" from 1977—written in four 12-line stanzas of variably indented lines, a hybridized New Sentence form—with rubbleized media language that echoed in our collective preconscious after 2016. Thus two moments of "language" are sampled for differing purposes. The original poem was itself sampled, from Lee Harwood's translation of Tristan Tzara, as lucid an example of automatic messaging as exists. The language of presentist media, on the other hand, telegraphs corruption and venality. In alternating lines from the original with their overwritten versions, as source to target, I wanted to compare two forms of automatism—poetic and ideological. Against the presentist distortion of ideological fantasy, the poem is dedicated to Tyrone Williams, who died during the preparation of this volume.

Sources: media; Tristan Tzara, *Selected Poems*, trans. Lee Harwood (Trigram Press, 1975); "Radio," in *1–10* (This, 1980).

Publications: "Radio," *ZZZZZZ* (ed. Kenward Elmslie; 1977); *1–10*; in *MAM.R.C. Bulletin littérature* (Paris; ed. Emmanuel Hocquard) no. 201 (1989); *Postmodern American Poetry: A Norton Anthology*, ed. Paul Hoover (Norton, 1995); *Frame (1971–1990)* (Sun & Moon, 1997); in "Barrett Watten," ed. Mañuel Brito, *Literatura norteamericana/American Poetry* (U Salamanca, Sp., 2007), online; correlation previously unpublished.

## [VIII]

### Notzeit (After Hannah Höch)

Notes: "Notzeit (After Hannah Höch)" was written over a five-week period, from 23 March to 26 April 2020. The first cases of COVID-19 in Michigan date from about March 6 but were not confirmed, due to lack of testing, until March 10—the night of the presidential primary. The weekend of 13–15 March saw a big increase in cases; on 13 March Wayne State University closed, initially for several weeks, and on 16 March Gov. Gretchen Whitmer closed bars and restaurants, issuing a stay-at-home order on 23 March. Confirmed cases and deaths in Michigan peaked about 30 March–1 April; at the poem's last entry there were about 60,000 cases and 6000 deaths.

On Monday, March 23, I had just completed a three-day "nonsite" seminar that was to have taken place at the ACLA conference in Chicago on March 20–22, titled "Modernity @ Zero Hour." Wanting to keep the focus on the concept of the "zero hour," I wrote the first dated entry of the poem under the title "Isolate Flecks," with an epigraph from Williams. I decided I would continue writing on a daily basis through the duration of our period of isolation, not knowing how long that would be, but with the requirement to add one more "stanza" of two run-over lines each day: on March 24, I wrote two stanzas; on March 25, three, and so on. As the work progressed, it became more difficult to write the required number of lines in one day. On 14 April I had to write twenty lines, which I was finding increasingly strenuous, beginning the section "Every day is one more, an increment." In order to keep up with the poem's demands, I sometimes had to write an entry over several days, and some days I had to skip due to fatigue—no lines would come. To get a line, I would think about nothing, recall my dreams from the night before, grab any book within reach and look for a prompt, or search randomly online.

The question then became how to end the poem, how long it could go on. I calculated the length of the poem using the formula for the sum of integers from 1 to n. If n is the number of days, the sum of lines would be $n(n+1)/2$. Writing n lines a day on each $day_n$ for 24 days give me a convenient total of 300 lines, matching my last long poem, "Plan B," which was written after the catastrophe of the 2016 election—except that the lines in "Plan B" are short, and I miscounted them (there are in fact 101 stanzas, or 303 lines). I found this too to be suggestive and finished the poem with the addition of a three-line stanza on day 25. After the first draft, I decided to change the title from Williams's well-known phrase (but keeping the epigraph), using the title of a watercolor series by the Dada artist Hannah Höch from her period of "inner emigration" in 1940s Berlin, sequestering in a small house and garden through the final days of the war. Höch's title means "Time of Suffering," but I like better the pun on duration: "Not Time." The concept of inner emigration, "going in," was a central concern in the writing of the poem.

But "going in" is also "going out" to determine whatever content is out there and can be meaningfully assembled in the poem. In the sections from 30 March–4 April, X–XIII (coinciding with the peak of the rise in cases and deaths, in fact), for example, materials include references to Höch, Williams's *Autobiography* (on his experience of the 1918 Spanish flu) and *Spring and All*, Lacan's seminar on anxiety, the journals of William L. Shirer as an American reporter in Berlin from the Munich accord to American entry into the war, a critical study on *On Interpretive Conflicts*, nightly TV series including *Freud* and *The Valhalla Murders*, and lists of symptoms (then known) of the virus. 1 April, in addition, coincided with the 2020 census, for which I entered "I who am here at this date and time, inhabiting this place with another"—Carla Harryman, with whom I shared the creative possibilities of sequestration.

As of 17 September 2021, date of the final draft of the poem, there have been 983,109 confirmed cases and 20,509 deaths, according to the Michigan coronavirus website. On 10 February 2023, with completion of the final MS for publication, there have been 3,036,304 confirmed and probable cases and 41,809 deaths in Michigan.

Sources: John Ashbery, *The Double Dream of Spring* and *A Wave*; Ted Berrigan, *The Sonnets* and *So Going Around Cities*; Joe Brainard, unattributed quote; André Breton, *Manifesto of Surrealism*, *Nadja*, and *The Communicating Vessels*; Dante, *Vita Nova* and *Purgatorio*; John Frow, *Conflicts of Interpretation*; George Floyd, Say Their Names; Hannah Höch, *Notzeit*, collages, and artist's statements; Mike Huckaby, RA Podcast 278; Ishi, "Tale of Wood Duck"; John Keats, "Sonnet VII. To My Brothers"; Jacques Lacan, *The Seminar*, book 10: *Anxiety*; Gérard de Nerval, *Aurélia*; Edgar Allan Poe, "The Philosophy of Composition"; Joseph Roth, *What I Saw*; Ryan Ruby, *Context Collapse*; Ridley Scott, dir., *Blade Runner*; William L. Shirer, *Berlin Diary*; Gertrude Stein, *Geography and Plays*; Denis Villeneuve, dir., *Blade Runner 2049*; Barrett Watten, *Decay*; William Carlos Williams, *Spring and All*, *The Autobiog-*

*raphy*, and *Selected Letters*; Ludwig Wittgenstein, *Philosophical Investigations*; contemporary media coverage of the pandemic; Monica Hesse, reportage on coronavirus dreams; streaming detective and crime series: *The Valhalla Murders, Deadwind, The Bridge, Babylon Berlin, Freud*; Michigan coronavirus website: http://michigan.gov/coronavirus.

Publications and readings: online posts as the poem was being written on Facebook; "Entry 40: Isolate Flecks," *barrettwatten.net* (23 March 2020), online; sections 10–13, with note, *Chants de la sirène* (ed. Laura Hinton) 2 (June 2020), online; section 18, YouTube recording available at https://bit.ly/2LZ1DQ6; section 19, *Poets Corner (Virtual Chautaqua)* (Greensburg [Ind.] High School, ed. John Pratt), YouTube recording available at https://bit.ly/3nETmPo; from *Notzeit (After Hannah Höch)*, trans. Ekaterina Zakharkhiv, with Stanislav Snitko, *Nosorog* (Rhinoceros; Moscow, St. Petersburg, Venice) 16 (Spring–Summer 2021); "Iz 'Notzeit (po Khanni Khokh),'" trans. Zakharkiv and Snitko, *Ot "chiornoi gori" do "yazikovo pisma": Antologiya noveishei poezii CShA* (From "Black Mountain" to "Language Writing": Anthology of New Poetry from the USA), ed. Vladimir Feshchenko and Ian Probstein (Novoe literaturnoye obozrenie [NLO], 2022). On Hannah Höch, see Watten, "Modernity @ Zero Hour: Three Women (Lee Miller, Hannah Höch, Anonyma)," in "Modernity @ Zero Hour: The Question of the Universal and the Origins of the Global Order," *Journal of Foreign Languages and Cultures* (Hunan Normal U) 4, no. 1 (June 2020).

## [IX]
### The Meridian as Archive

Notes: In 2020, Russian poet Ivan Sokolov asked me if I might contribute a work for an online russophone publication commemorating the centennial of Paul Celan's birth. I decided to make a work assembling responses to Pierre Joris's translation of "The Meridian" and its drafts and fragments as an archive of translation, travel, and Celan's poetics. To elucidate the poem I paired it with Friedrich Hölderlin's "Hälfte des Lebens," itself a meridian of the German lyric. Sokolov translated half the work, and then uploaded the original in an online supplement. I decided, as well, that my archive of Celan would be ten sections of ten numbered sentences each, which I distributed among the poem's various sources.

Sources: Paul Celan, *The Meridian: Final Version–Drafts–Materials*, trans. Pierre Joris (Stanford UP, 2011); Robert Creeley, "Numbers," *Collected Poems, 1945–1975* (U California P, 1982); Friedrich Hölderlin, "Hälfte des Lebens," *Hymns and Fragments*, trans. Richard

Sieburth (Princeton UP, 1986); *Selected Poems and Fragments*, trans. Michael Hamburger (Penguin, 2007).

Publications: "Meridian kak arkhiv" (The Meridian as Archive), trans. Ivan Sokolov, *Tselan perklyiuchaya stoletie* (Celan Switching Centuries), part 1, ed. Sokolov, Anna Glazova, and Galina Rymbu, *Grioza* (Dream; November 2020), online; "The Meridian as Archive," parts 1–5, in *Celan: Leaping the Cent(u/ena)ry (Celan: Jahrhundertschalten; Celan: En commutat le siècle/centenaire),* "A digest of nonrussophone submissions in the originals," part 1, ed. Sokolov and Glazova, *Grioza.*

## [X]
## Unthought

Notes: In 2018, Polish poet Marcin Sendecki asked if I could contribute a work for an anthology celebrating the writings of Stanislav Lem. I responded with enthusiasm: "I would very much like to do something for your project, so will take out my Lem. I know *Solaris* through Tarkovsky—it is a 'prime' text for me—but not the novel. But at the same time I am very much interested in other projects that take off from Lem, such as the *Blade Runner* series. I based a recent graduate seminar on the theoretical implications of *Blade Runner 2049*." COVID added a dimension to the experience of the film as well. I wrote the poem over a weekend in April 2021. The poem takes a single sentence from Lem as lexia and unpacks it over ten stanzas of twenty lines each. In addition to sampling the novel and film, the poem incorporates current reading from N. Katherine Hayles, from whom I took the title, as well as two works concerning Displaced Persons after World War II: Céline's novels of disgraced exile and Rossellini's docu-cinema tragedy *Stromboli.*

Sources: Stanislaw Lem, *Solaris*, trans. Joanna Kilmartin and Steve Cox (Harcourt, 1970); *Solaris*, dir. Andrei Tarkovsky (1972); N. Katherine Hayles, *Unthought: The Power of the Cognitive Nonconscious* (U Chicago P, 2017); Louis-Ferdinand Céline, *Castle to Castle*, trans. Ralph Manheim (1957; Dalkey Archive, 1997); Ingrid Bergman, *Stromboli*, dir. Roberto Rossellini (1950); notebooks.

Publication: previously unpublished.

## [XI]
### Orphée in Translation

Notes: Like *Solaris*, Cocteau's *Orphée* is a primary film, for many poets one might add. My enthusiasm for the work has been difficult to communicate and I have never found a way to add it to the "rotation" in teaching. About 2016 I returned to watching it intensively, particularly for the backward unfolding of object and desire. To write the poem I correlated notes from multiple viewings, caught lines in French, and an online translation of the entire script, which I sampled using random techniques. My rule was to translate from one to three lines into French, checking my work with online translators such as DeepL, for each of 100 four-line stanzas. Translation is happening on multiple levels—language, history, experience—correlating, for instance, Bill Berkson (photographed at an outdoor café table of poets at Spoleto in 1965) with Jean Marais at the Café des poètes. The deathward film rhymes with its life-giving clarity, in my reading, strictly on the faultline of the (im)possibility of desired ends. It is the form of life in the zone between. The poem was completed during the late COVID period, over three days in July 2021. As a work in defense of poetry, it could not possibly be dedicated to anyone.

Sources: *Orphée*, dir. Jean Cocteau (1950); online English script; notebooks.

Publication: previously unpublished.

## [XII]
### Some / Ruins

Notes: I have always found significant the "eidetic word"—the "word way back in the head," after Robert Grenier but also Surrealism—and have attended to it. In a period of chiasmus in fall 2019, prior to COVID, with normative structures unplugged and forms of mass hysteria replacing them, I would spontaneously record in my notebook minimal pairs of words, usually prompted by a dominant, anticipatory word that I would print in CAPS and a regressive, retrospective word that would answer it, upper and lower case. These pairings are primitive poems across a faultline where a preconscious word erupts and returns in an echo of itself. As language, these minimal pairs recall the binary theories of Roman Jakobson; some recent work in linguistics sees such binary combinations, "below the level of the sentence" or "non-sentential," as fossils of the evolution of language. As linguistic atavisms or cognitive ruins, they correlated well with my experience at the time. I printed 128 pairs out on 4 x 6" index cards, culled and arranged them in groups of four to emphasize their chiasmic nature, and reproduce them here. They recall the method of Grenier's *Sentences*, his 500 index cards with short poems in nonproportional font, also known as "The Box," at a later moment. They are also informed by the next generation Voight-Kampff test Joe K performs in *Blade Runner 2049*, as a system check on his cognitive function.

Source: notebooks.

Publication: previously unpublished.

## [Credits]

Front cover: Joanna Buchowska, "whenever i put them." 40x40 cm, various paper, acrylic, ink, marker on canvas. Courtesy Martin Mertens Gallery, Berlin; © 2025 Artists Rights Society (ARS), New York/VG Bild Kunst, Bonn.

Back cover: Etel Adnan, from *Shifting the Silence* (Nightboat Books, 2020), 52; used by permission of Simone Fattal; Lyn Hejinian, from *The Book of a Thousand Eyes* (Omnidawn, 2012), 71; used by permission of the Estate of Lyn Hejinian.

Back cover photo: author (2025).

Epigraphs: from "Silence," in *1–10* (*This*, 1980); *Frame* (1971–1990), 35; Alexander Kluge, "The Difference: Heinrich Kleist," in *Difference and Orientation: An Alexander Kluge Reader*, ed. Richard Langston (Cornell UP, 2019), 29, 30.

## About the Author

Barrett Watten's concept of "zone" has many sources. One extends back to his boyhood in Taiwan, a zone of its own, poised between China and Japan, with sea all around. That early space between has a bearing on his lifelong exploration of zones of thought, zones of language, zones of conflict. As a poet, he emerges out of Robert Creeley, Ted Berrigan, Joanne Kyger, and Anselm Hollo, onward to Robert Grenier and Clark Coolidge, Gertrude Stein and Louis Zukofsky, and into community with the Language poets and their theoretical biographies around a Grand Piano. He moves through various frames or zones of discovery as we might move through counties and states and decades, all the while staying on edge, at once dramatic, funny, and exacting. I can't quite imagine writing a true biography of Barrett Watten, but I can imagine walking with him across those edges, moving progress and bad history under erasure into and out of those frames and zones.

Professor of English at Wayne State University, leader of an entire wave of "newer" American poetries from the 1970s to the present, in cohort with leading lights such as Carla Harryman, Lyn Hejinian, Ron Silliman, Kit Robinson, Steve Benson, Ted Pearson and more than can be named here. Watten as scholar, Watten as poet, Watten as a force invites our attention and rewards it tenfold.

## About Chax

Founded in 1984 in Tucson, Arizona, Chax has published more than 250 books in a variety of formats, including hand printed letterpress books and chapbooks, hybrid chapbooks, book arts editions, and trade paperback editions such as the book you are holding. From August 2014 until July 2018 Chax Press resided in the University of Houston-Victoria Downtown Center for the Arts. Chax is a nonprofit 501c3 organization which depends on suppport from various government & private funders, and, primarly, from individual donors and readers. In July 2018 Chax Press returned to Tucson. In 2021, Chax Press founder and director Charles Alexander was awarded the Lord Nose Award for lifetime achievement in literary publishing. In January 2024 Chax established a new studio for its letterpress printing and book arts work, and in July 2025 begins a new education project that will include classes on literary topics, creative writing workshops, book arts workshops, and a variety of lectures and discussions.

Chax Press stands against all attacks on democracy, civil rights, and the dignity and self-determination of all peoples, in the USA and internationally. We stand against authoritarian government, including that which exists within supposedly democratic systems. We stand against racism and misogyny, and against all genocides, including the one being enacted presently in Gaza against the Palestinian people. We stand for equal human rights for all, and we encourage and believe in peace and love as critical to solving problems in our world.

Your support of our projects as a reader, and as a benefactor, is much appreciated. Our current mailing address is 6181 East 4th Street, Tucson, Arizona 85711-1613. You can email us at *chaxpress@chax.org*. Find CHAX online at *https://chax.org*.

This book has been designed by Charles Alexander, with the assistance of Barrett Watten. Printing services by IPG (Independent Publishers Group). The fonts used are Minion Pro and Gill Sans.